Literature of the Lost Home

KOBAYASHI HIDEO—
LITERARY CRITICISM,
1924–1939

LITERATURE OF THE LOST HOME

KOBAYASHI HIDEO—
Literary Criticism,
1924–1939

EDITED AND TRANSLATED AND
WITH AN INTRODUCTION BY

PAUL ANDERER

Stanford University Press
Stanford, California

Stanford University Press
Stanford, California

The essays included in this volume were
originally published in Japanese and are
translated and published here by permission.
Hideo Kobayashi
KOBAYASHI HIDEO CHOSAKUSHU
Copyright © Haruko Shirasu
Originally published in Japan

Printed in the United States of America

CIP data appear at the end of the book

Acknowledgments

For their generosity and support, I thank the National Endowment for the Humanities, the Fulbright Commission, and the Social Science Research Council, as well as the staff of Columbia's Starr East Asian Library and of the Kindai Bungakkan in Tokyo.

Many colleagues and friends, by their practical advice or commitment to the project, helped me along the way. They include Asada Akira, William Currie, S.J., Judy Geib, Hasumi Shigehiko, Hosea Hirata, Donald Keene, the late Nakagami Kenji, Thomas Rimer, Sabu Kohso, Naoki Sakai, Edward Seidensticker, Shimada Masahiko, Haruo Shirane, William Sibley, Suga Hidemi, Tomi Suzuki, Watanabe Naomi, Yamada Kenji, Yomota Inuhiko, and Yoshimoto Takaaki. I am indebted to them all, as I am to an extraordinary group of graduate students at Columbia, who over several years read and reacted to Kobayashi and helped clarify my thinking about him.

For their detailed, illuminating responses to my questions about Kobayashi's critical achievements and his prose, I owe much to Etō Jun, Karatani Kōjin, and Miura Masashi. Ken Ito read the entire manuscript with acuity and care; his judgments and his friendship are deeply appreciated. At Stanford University Press, my editors Helen Tartar and John Ziemer offered encouragement and patient advice at every stage.

An earlier version of the translation of one essay, "Literature of the Lost Home," appeared in *New Leaves: Studies and Translations of Japanese Literature in Honor of Edward Seidensticker*, edited by Aileen Gatten and Anthony Hood Chambers, Michigan Monograph Series in Japanese Studies no. 11 (Ann Arbor: Center for Japanese Studies, University of Michigan, 1993), pp. 175–83. © 1993 Center for Japanese Studies, University of Michigan. Used by permission.

My family makes this and all my work merely possible. I am grateful beyond measure to my wife, Mia, and to our sons, Erich, Nicholas, and Peter.

I dedicate this book to my teacher, Edwin McClellan.

P.A.

Contents

Contents

REFERENCE MATTER

Literature of the Lost Home

KOBAYASHI HIDEO—
LITERARY CRITICISM,
1924–1939

Introduction

Kobayashi Hideo (1902–83) was a literary critic—reviewer, essayist, observer of the shifting shape of modern cultural life—who in turn shaped Japanese literature in the twentieth century. His stature approaches that of such novelists as Natsume Sōseki or Tanizaki Jun'ichirō,[1] that is, the greatest writers of modern Japan. By any standard, Kobayashi was the pivotal Japanese critic of his time, as crucial a presence in his own literary culture as, for example, Edmund Wilson, Walter Benjamin, or Roland Barthes have been in their own.

Born and educated in Tokyo after the first wave of contact with the West, he lived amid transformation, within a translation culture where, as he once remarked, the Moroccan desert seen at the movies appeared closer than the Ginza street before one's eyes. Kobayashi's early work especially represents a stubborn, skeptical exploration of French, Russian, and contemporary Japanese literature, revealing the historical, stylistic discriminations that an active critic must make, and in light of which mere labels—romantic, naturalist, symbolist, social realist—fade away. Here, every academic or political tendency to classify, and hence to define or solve literary problems, is resisted. What surfaces instead is the questioning and self-questioning style of the critic as he explores

1. See the Glossary for identification of many writers and terms that appear in this text.

such singular historical figures as Rimbaud, Gide, Dostoevsky, and Shiga Naoya; the faces of these authors as they appear reflected in the critic's own face; the exertions of consciousness in its struggle with hybrid, extraterritorial realities; the play of the spirit in writing.

In Kobayashi's early work, many have found the beginnings of literary criticism in modern Japan. Etō Jun's postwar, Sartrean evaluation of his predecessor captures a prevailing sentiment: "It is not that there were no critics before Kobayashi. But there were no critics conscious of themselves as critics before him. This is only to say that for Kobayashi, self-consciousness meant being conscious of the act of criticism as a problem of his very existence."[2]

The literary world Kobayashi entered in the late 1920's teemed with critical controversy. It could even be called an age of criticism, of cultural thought experiments that would not survive the 1930's and its insistent, more univocal demands. Yet throughout this period—the historical locus of this book and its translations—Kobayashi regularly called into question any fixed ideological position or "design," in particular those advocated by ideologues who seemed incapable of self-criticism or, worse, who showed no awareness of the tension and paradox that line both literature and its evaluation.

It was Kobayashi's fundamental insight that criticism is expressive, baring through its forms and arguments the values and tastes of the critic; in other words, that criticism could itself be a style of literature. Yet in modern Japan, where literary values and tastes were subject to incessant change and exaggeration, to the latest breaking wave of translated literature and reflexive response, Kobayashi remained skeptical of the apparent stability of any announced position, whether Marxist, aestheticist, or nationalist, especially where these positions were conveyed impersonally, as a dunning recitation of preselected facts or theories. Criticism, as Kobayashi demonstrated by his own practice, should instead be an exploration of consciousness, a matter of internal urgency, motivated less by general conditions of the world or even by habits of

2. Etō, *Kobayashi Hideo*, p. 8. For similar statements, see Aeba, *Kobayashi Hideo to sono jidai*, p. 321; also Nakamura, *Kobayashi Hideo shū*, pp. 484–85.

mind than by a specific provocation, a question that demands a personal response.

In the 1930's, after the government moved to censor and ban proletarian writing, Kobayashi, a sharp critic of vulgar Marxism, maintained his distance from the new movement to distill a "pure" Japanese culture from a mixture of native and Western or outside influences. There is an unmistakable tone of nostalgia in his reflections on the culturally homeless condition of modern, urban Japanese. But there is a recognition, too, that the lost home is an actuality to be experienced and not obscured in romantic pursuit of the true Japan or the dubious revival of an imagined Japanese purity.

By the 1940's Kobayashi had moved away from contemporary literature toward studies or appreciations of the classics, although his embrace remained expansive, drawing in Minamoto Sanetomo and Mozart, van Gogh and Motoori Norinaga. He seemed devoted especially to the elegiac writings of medieval Japan, a period of warfare and cultural upheaval resembling his own, and to its poets and storytellers for their lyrical but stoic, Buddhist regard for the passing tragedy of desire and worldly ambition. In no sense did his wartime writings represent resistance literature—there was no such writing to speak of throughout the period of imperial aggression. But neither was Kobayashi a crude apologist for the military or Japanese expansionism, as were some whose revolutionary convictions had long since failed to sustain their opposition to the state. His classical studies, far less turbulent and paradox-riven than his earlier work, reveal a critic wearying of his century. Yet this work too might be read as part of Kobayashi's continuing attempt to register his response to the culture of modern urban life, which by turns denies, invents, or finds refuge in the past.

And so even present-day Japanese critics of pronounced theoretical interests, who clearly mean to move beyond Kobayashi, acknowledge that modern literary criticism in Japan properly begins with him.[3] It is a complicated admission, not least for its apparent dismissal of pre-existing critical or evaluative practices. To be sure, there are millennium-old traditions of commentary and textual

3. See, e.g., Karatani and Nakagami, *Kobayashi Hideo o koete.*

scholarship in Japan, chiefly devoted to poetry, as well as manuals
on literary or theatrical technique, including work of such distinction as Kamo no Chōmei's *Mumyōshō* or Zeami Motokiyo's *Ka-
densho*. There is Motoori Norinaga, the great eighteenth-century
scholar of National Learning and the subject of a monumental
study by Kobayashi, who explored tensions in Japanese literature—
between speech and writing, the native and the (Chinese) other,
feeling and ideology—that startlingly anticipate some of the central issues addressed by literati in the Meiji period (1868–1912).

Indeed, critical activity had increased dramatically by the
1880's, a conventional starting date for "modern Japanese literature." This was coincident with the formation, both material and
ideological, of the nation-state and the invention of a new literary
language—*genbun itchi*—calculated to admit common speech into
fictional prose and so to portray the modern world "as it is." Criticism, *bungei hihyō*, became the agency that debated, encoded, or
classified Western literatures and consequently determined anew
the boundaries and traits of a native "Japanese" literature—*kokubungaku*. In this way it emerged with the novel as the dominant
genre of the post–Meiji Restoration age.

However else we characterize or date modernity in Japan, we
can say that it signifies a heightened cross-cultural and intra-
cultural struggle among several narratives for representation. And
so it should surprise only the most rearguard Orientalist, convinced that Japan is an exotic land of feeling and not of thought,
that criticism would emerge as a quintessential form of modern
Japanese writing.[4]

Still, the retrospective claim that Kobayashi was the "first
critic" might seem puzzling in this historical light. For we encounter a massive volume of published literary debates, position papers,
stylistic analyses, and genre theories produced after Meiji Japan's
first exposure to Western literature. These range from Tsubouchi
Shōyō's defense of realism in the novel to Mori Ōgai's idealist conception of literary art as a special world of beauty; from Yamaji Aizan's utilitarianism to Kitamura Tōkoku's romantic retreat into
the transcendental sublime. It includes the textual criticism of the

---

4. See *Kindai bungaku hyōron taikei*, 1: 465, for Yoshida Seiichi's authori-
tative statement on the matter.

German scholar Ishibashi Ningetsu or of Uchida Roan (who was also a translator, notably of Dostoevsky's *Crime and Punishment*); Natsume Sōseki's ambitious, rhetoric-based *Bungakuron* (Theory of literature); and the volley of doctrinaire statements that ushered in Japanese Naturalism at the turn of the century, emphasizing plainspoken or confessional truths over literary craft.[5]

By 1910, the emergence of such influential literary magazines as *Mita bungaku*, *Shinshichō*, and *Shirakaba* seemed to inaugurate a new era of cultural self-confidence, something distantly glimpsed by the earlier Meiji generation of scholars, editors, and writers, whose own formidable linguistic and literary accomplishments nevertheless were shadowed by a sense of their own "late development" by Western, Darwinian cultural standards. Thus at the beginning of the Taishō period (1912–25), in the name of sensibility or self-expression, and following victory in wars against both China and Russia, a dizzying array of imported or homegrown flowers of high culture began to bloom. A modern, international culture was cultivated with élan, if in hothouse isolation from the outside and still Euro-centered world.

Van Gogh was discovered at this time—a marvelous irony given the artist's own discovery of "Japan" a quarter of a century earlier—his self-sacrifice for art being seen as somehow more modern and comprehensible than General Nogi's feudal action of following the Meiji emperor in death. In a period given to theatrical gestures, Ibsen, Maeterlinck, Strindberg, and Chekhov were lionized. Tolstoy and Whitman were described as giants of humanism, as outsized as Russia and America and equally untamed by European codes of cultural conduct. Iwano Hōmei's translation of Arthur Symons's *The Symbolist Movement in Literature* helped stimulate a whole range of disturbingly experimental styles: decadence, dilettantism, surrealism, dadaism, and futurism. Nagai Kafū, after his discovery of things Japanese in France, went on to locate his *fleurs du mal* in the Edo past. There appeared, too, a certain action-oriented poetics, drawing on Marx, the Swedish feminist Ellen Key, and the Russian prince-turned-anarchist Piotr Kropotkin, that doubtless served as a basis for Ōsugi Sakae's attachment to the energy-rich proletariat

5. See *Kindai bungaku hyōron taikei*, vols. 1–3, for a standard edition of representative Meiji criticism.

and a people's art and Hiratsuka Raichō's feminist vision of a pri-
meval sun-woman, too long kept in the shadow of the mere moon-
light of man.[6]

It was, withal, a heady, cosmopolitan, eerily postmodern time,
whose openness to everything may have simply been, as the poet/
critic Ishikawa Takuboku saw it, a sign of mass confusion, careless
terms and judgments, cultural narcissism, or nation-family-self-
enclosure.[7] It was, we should note, the period of Kobayashi's own
upbringing. He was, in other words, a Taishō literary youth.

Kobayashi's first major work of criticism, "Samazama naru
ishō" (Multiple designs) was published in the September 1929 issue
of *Kaizō* (Reconstruction), an established monthly whose origins
lay in the eclectic agitations that marked the latter half of the
Taishō era. Kobayashi had studied French literature at Tokyo University and, while a student there, began to publish studies and
translations of Baudelaire, Rimbaud, and Gide in small, coterie
magazines. He became a private tutor of French; the post–World
War II novelist Ōoka Shōhei numbered among his pupils. Indeed,
Kobayashi's training in French bears witness to an evolving hierar-
chy of taste. By the mid-1920's French culture had been identified
as the center of high European modernism and so an exemplary
subject of study, at least for students of literature at elite universi-
ties.

When "Multiple Designs" appeared, bringing Kobayashi immediate acclaim and instant visibility in the literary world, the scene
was dominated by Marxist critics, apologists for social realism in
the novel and historical materialism in cultural studies. One such
critic was Miyamoto Kenji, whose "Haiboku no bungaku" (Literature of defeat), a treatise on Akutagawa's aberrant if poignant writings and suicidal end, took first prize in the essay competition
sponsored by *Kaizō*. Given the literary politics of the time, Kobayashi's more powerful "Designs" was consigned to second place.

Even before Kobayashi, Marxist theory and practice had not
gone unchallenged. The modernists associated with the Shinkan-
kaku (Neo-Perceptionist) School, including Yokomitsu Riichi and

6. Ibid., vols. 4–5.
7. Ishikawa, "Jidai heisoku no genjō."

the young Kawabata Yasunari, hewed to experimental practices calculated to record the speed and disjunctiveness of city life, and were not bound by the strictures of ameliorative social analysis. And various bourgeois writers pressed their right to remain indifferent to class issues. Yet it was to these groups no less than the Marxists, concerned as they all were to classify poems and stories by political allegiance or by resemblance to a favorite Western method or model, that Kobayashi's essay issued a challenge. The personal, ironic tone of the style alone constituted an attack on cultural naiveté and ideological complacency. It also uncovered the critic as the heretofore hidden but proper subject of criticism.

No one before Kobayashi had brought this measure of self-consciousness to Japanese criticism. Still, the subjective agency that informs "Multiple Designs" makes no frontal assault on universalist theory or on deterministic ideological positions. As if to build a defense against determinism into his writing itself, Kobayashi rejected a neutral, rationalist idiom in favor of paradox and indirection. In trying to convey the reality of his encounter with a specific work or controversy, he moved with often sudden recognition toward the spiritual, magical aspects of cultural engagement. In this, he acknowledged a debt to Baudelaire:

> At such moments, captivated by Baudelaire's verbal magic, I see with utter clarity the formal contours neither of his taste nor of his intellectual standards. I see only his dreams that have taken the form of an unparalleled passion. This is justifiably called criticism; it could as well be called a soliloquy. Some have tried variously to separate criticism and self-consciousness. But the magical power of Baudelaire's criticism derives from his awareness that to write criticism is to make oneself conscious. To say that the subject of criticism is the self and the other is to say that there is but a single subject, not two. For is not criticism finally the skeptical narration of our dreams?[8]

What Kobayashi brought to Japanese critical practice was a certain double vision, a way of looking outward at the work in question and inward at the critic's subjective response. What is illuminated, becoming clear as a "single subject," conjoins, then, both external and internal conditions, personal and social values, so that

8. Kobayashi, "Samazama naru ishō," pp. 26–27.

any theory or design that would seek to elevate one value and sup-
press the other must be seen as reducing the scope of literature and
the possibilities of literary criticism.

Kobayashi's critical attention turned inevitably toward the "I-
novel" or fiction of the self—*watakushi shōsetsu*—the dominant
mode of serious fiction writing since the turn of the twentieth century in Japan. Even the social realists of the 1920's and the 1930's
frequently wrote their stories, set in mines or fisheries or factories,
in the key of a personal confession. Whereas much critical or bio-
graphical commentary assumed a seamless equivalence between
the author of an I-novel and its fictional protagonist, Kobayashi
regularly probed for the distances, as well as for signs of possible
connection, between literature and reality, autobiography and art,
or empirical and fictional character. And so he observes in "Discourse on Fiction of the Self," his famous culminating statement
on this most pervasive literary style,

> Authors may not really choose what they write about, nor do
> they imagine that their way of writing itself might become the
> subject of their work. Yet such unimagined things regularly oc-
> cur. It is the case that writers are controlled in the very process of
> writing—their style becomes the subject of their work—and so
> they must create literature of a specific kind. What provides the
> truly essential material is not reality but a way of seeing reality,
> or a way of thinking about it.[9]

Such questions of individual or artistic identity may seem
quaint or misguided to those who theorize that the "self," no less
than the "author," is a pathological delusion of Western origin or is
simply passé and dead. But the historical record shows that these
very questions have animated Japanese cultural life throughout the
twentieth century. The great novelist Natsume Sōseki was himself
in middle age when he transcribed in *Sanshirō* (1908) the modern
story of a country youth coming of age amid the confusions and
treacheries of the city, thereby contributing a character to what
was becoming an archetypal and widely emulated figure both in
fiction and life: the *bungaku seinen* or "literary youth," uneasy and
displaced, a "self" with something to confess.

9. Kobayashi, "Watakushi shōsetsu ron," pp. 135–36.

Of course Sōseki's characters reflect their author's ethical resistance to excessive self-absorption, to bookish rather than real-life experience. Other writers would feature a similarly troubled but more solipsistic youth, whose life remains sordid or impoverished until ennobled by literary confession. The genre that would become known as *watakushi shōsetsu*, whether falling under the shadow of a seedy Naturalist confession or within the dawn-breaking hopefulness of Shirakaba School accounts of self-recovery, prevailed throughout the Taishō period. It was sustained by writers and readers who identified with "literary youth," that is, with literary characters who often resembled themselves. Indeed, the omnipresence of personal fiction and the *bungaku seinen* archetype helped sharpen the point of Marxist criticism; namely, that the evils of subjectivism were everywhere to be found in Japanese culture and society.

Kobayashi, too, observed the severe constraints imposed on Japanese fiction by the *watakushi shōsetsu*. He distinguished between the "socialized self" of Rousseau's *Confessions* and the more isolated selves of Japanese confessionalists, uncovering no innate differences between French and Japanese practices, only formal or historical ones. Yet Kobayashi remained wary of mechanistic, class-conscious criticism because of its denial that personality or individual desire could shape either fiction or ideas. Quoting Marx (*The German Ideology*) against certain Marxists, he subscribed to a belief that consciousness is nothing other than existence made conscious, going on to explore the possibility that a fiction of the self could embrace ideas, society, and the world, but only if it broke out of the frame of a doctrinaire criticism or dogmatic fictional practice.

> I care neither for the phrase "art for the proletariat" nor for the phrase "art for art's sake." As rhetoric, such expressions are variously colorful, but in the end speak to nothing substantial. Which is more difficult: to fight for one's country or for oneself? It sounds simple to tell someone to make art for the proletariat or to make art for art's sake, but the artist so instructed is equally vexed.
>
>   . . . An individual's ideology is bound up with his total existence. It is tied to an individual's fate. Because a certain lassitude is also part of being human, one should find nothing objection-

able about a given writer's indifference to ideology. However, when we realize that what generates ideology is not in every instance theory but the forces of human life, then ideology becomes a part of our reality. And although we may not be interested in a particular aspect of reality, we cannot afford to scorn what is real.[10]

Much of Kobayashi's early work, whether focused on a fiction of the self, cultural homelessness, or the ideological chaos and cultural anxieties afflicting Japan in the 1930's, begins in anecdotal, almost colloquial defiance of reductive classification schemes, of pat literary slogans and jargon-strewn arguments. His own tack is to investigate, rather than define, specific literary phenomena, and so he uses a style marked by paradox and self-questioning. Still, the overall effect is not of random, subjective jottings, but of a "drama of consciousness," as the critic Akiyama Susumu has called it, played out according both to chance and fate—existential necessity.[11] This is what Kobayashi discovered in Shiga Naoya, an author of personal fiction whom he revered; namely, that literature is shaped by the "destiny" that each writer must discover within, not in a borrowed method or in detached observation of real life.

Much of Kobayashi's early writing might be seen as tracing the images and character types produced by his identity-obsessed youth culture. Although the youth culture is often regarded as a Taishō phenomenon, an early version of it had surfaced by the 1880's, when the failure of the People's Rights movement and the imposition of a restrictive constitution turned some from politics toward art (even those whose stated goal was to reject art and write more "realistically") and toward a world, however risk-provoking, of the imagination. From this time, Japanese writers began declaring with considerable certitude what literature is, in relation to a given genre or national culture. And here we locate the origins of Kobayashi's complaint; namely, that earlier critics did not question the grounds of their assurance:

Have these general complications within the modern critical spirit cast any sort of shadow over literary criticism in our country? We cannot find them, for example, in the criticism of Mori

10. Kobayashi, "Samazama naru ishō," p. 31.
11. See Akiyama in Yoshida, *Rekuwiemu Kobayashi Hideo*, p. 152.

Ōgai, the greatest of our importers of Western writing. . . . We would witness [Takayama] Chogyū's intoxication with Nietzsche, [Shimamura] Hōgetsu's application of Arnold, [Ueda] Bin's emulation of Pater. Yet amid all this critical activity, no one questioned what made a literary work "literary."[12]

Quite deliberately, Kobayashi took up the charge presented by this historical legacy as if it were his personal fate. He posed questions that had gone unasked in his modern culture, beginning with a basic question: What is literature?

These interrogations, which mark the style and concerns of all his early criticism, led Kobayashi to conclude that by the 1880's and through a flood of English, French, German, and Russian translations, Japanese literature had already moved beyond self-evident definitions of what a poem or a novel simply is or should be. Moreover, given the continuing transformations in education, publishing, and the conception of literature throughout the subsequent Taishō period and well into the 1930's, Kobayashi insisted that it was no longer possible to distinguish "foreign" literature from Japanese writing, as if these were fixed and separable categories. Instead, he engaged the hybrid, illusionary texture of Japan's modernity, which both occasioned and confirmed the stylistic traits and interrogatory disposition that distinguish his early writing. It was his very grasp of twentieth-century culture that moved Kobayashi to question anything stated in the name of a committee or a school, the latest theory or imported icon.

Not surprisingly, Kobayashi's questions often circle around the youth culture itself, which had in a sense commandeered Japanese literature, filling it with all manner of translated obsessions, political dogmas, and, especially in the 1930's, nativist ideals. Kobayashi cites the early Romantic turned Naturalist Kunikida Doppo's "possession" by Wordsworth as a local example of a phenomenon prevalent since the turn of the century: "Every Japanese writer . . . worked in the grip of his own Wordsworth. Each had his own beloved Wordsworth, or Zola, or Maupassant, or Flaubert."[13] Such possessions seemed only to intensify, with the consolidation of oligarchic power and the political lockout that followed the Russo-Japanese War. The Taishō period, for all its cosmopolitan veneer

12. Kobayashi, "Bungakkai no konran," p. 89.
13. Kobayashi, "Watakushi shōsetsu ron," p. 110.

and international frame of reference, was also markedly involuted and decadent, an era of emporiums and movie houses where foreign brand names and exotic types were fetishized and domesticated on an ever wider screen, on a mass and consumer-culture scale, that far eclipsed Doppo's quiet devotion to the English poet. It was a condition observed and wickedly exploited by the young Tanizaki, whose femmes fatales crush their prey with a Mary Pickford smile or a drag on a Dimitrino Slim.[14]

Kobayashi's criticism begins, then, with a wary backward glance and perduring anxiety over the self-absorbed youth culture within which he had himself been raised and which, in defiance of passing time, still existed in the culture around him. Regardless of school or league or coterie affiliation, the literati whom Kobayashi challenged were like ageless youth, caught in the grip of fixed, if paradoxically fleeting, images of self and society. Small wonder that the foreign writer who most possessed Kobayashi throughout the 1930's was Dostoevsky, or that he would consciously link this Russian writer to his critique of youth culture, which was also, of course, a self-critique:

> The other day, rereading Dostoevsky's *Raw Youth* in the Yonekawa Masao translation, I was struck by several things that had not occurred to me when I first read the book. In particular, I sensed the importance of the title chosen by the author. Illuminating the world seen by a single youth through the language of a single youth, the author revealed all the attributes of youth in general: its beauty and ugliness, hypersensitivity and insensibility, madness and passion and absurdity—in short, its authentic shape. I was left with an almost unbearably strong feeling that it is incorrect to call young people "youth." They are, rather, a species of animal that must be called by some other name. It struck me too that Dostoevsky's youth is no stranger—a youth whose mind is in turmoil because of Western ideas and who, in the midst of this intellectual agitation, has utterly lost his home. How very closely he resembles us. Indeed, I repeatedly ran into scenes that made me feel that the author was describing me, that he had me firmly in his grasp.[15]

Here, in "Literature of the Lost Home," Kobayashi explores modern Tokyo, the city of his birth, not for superficial signs of re-

14. See esp. Tanizaki, *Chijin no ai* (tr. as *Naomi*).
15. Kobayashi, "Kokyō o ushinatta bungaku," pp. 72–73.

semblance to St. Petersburg, but for a "reality" analogous to the one seen and recorded by Dostoevsky, of phantasms and illusions walking the city streets: "I do not easily recognize within myself or in the world around me people whose feet are planted firmly on the ground, or who have the features of social beings. I can more easily recognize the face of that abstraction called the 'city person,' who might have been born anywhere, than a Tokyoite born in the city of Tokyo."[16]

This characteristic statement of Kobayashi's discontent nevertheless does not reject outright the modern world or deny its own reality. Neither would Kobayashi fully embrace the romantic, nationalist flights toward Nature, village life, and tradition, collectively coded as a "return to Japan," that were so powerful a part of intellectual life in the 1930's and through the war years. Instead he saw them as further symptoms of a culture driven spasmodically to change course or direction, like a stranger lost and lurching through the streets of a suddenly unfamiliar city.

As Karatani Kōjin has argued, Kobayashi did not succumb to the "revival" of traditional Japanese aesthetics in the 1930's, nor did he recognize the "guiding principles" of a narrowly nationalist literary culture in the early 1940's.[17] Because he had not earlier embraced Marxism, there was nothing for Kobayashi to recant under government pressure. Lapsed leftists remained attached to the "people," no longer reified as the proletariat or the masses, but reconstituted as the simple folk. Yasuda Yojūrō and the Romantic school spun intricate "dreams of difference" about a Japan that might transcend universal, European models of the modern. Yet such dreams, however beautiful and ironic ("difference" itself emerging via the German Romantics), were seldom part of Kobayashi's consciousness or sense of attachment.[18]

Indeed, at least through the 1930's, Kobayashi persistently immersed himself in the modern world. This provoked anxiety, to be sure, even a sense of chaos wrought by slogans masquerading as political principles or by literati committed to revolutionary ideas prior to interrogation but, afterward, to "purer" Japanese thoughts.

16. Ibid., pp. 71–72.

17. See, e.g., *Issatsu no kōza—Kobayashi Hideo*, p. 35; also Karatani et al., *Kindai Nihon no hihyō*, p. 129.

18. On Yasuda and the Romantic school, see Doak, *Dreams of Difference*, esp. p. xxxv.

Modernity was for him an atmosphere, thick with whirling abstractions and images generated by the displacements of city life,
which the critic recognized and explored as the proper ground of his
culture's condition. One measure of Kobayashi's acuity and
strength as a critic is that he detected patterns within much that
barely cohered or emerged misshapen under pressure of outside influence and internal response; and further, that he saw through
these patterns, into the irreducible actuality of modern Japanese
cultural life.

   That Kobayashi has been called the "first critic" of modern Japan or has been described variously as the "god of criticism" or as
"a craggy mountain sending out vibrations into every area of modern Japanese literature" (by no less an iconoclast than Nakagami
Kenji) is perhaps reason enough to read him.[19] Another is the issue
of representation. Western methods of interpretation and commentary should remain available to any critic of Japanese literature, in
recognition of their historical place in modern Japanese intellectual life, if not also as a measure of critical freedom. But surely, too,
we must engage Japanese criticism itself, because of its centrality
to modern Japanese literature. In important respects, what is modern about Japanese literature is as vividly conveyed by its criticism
as by any experimental poem, novel, or play. Throughout the twentieth century, successive generations of Japanese critics, some
more insightfully than others, have presented a range of arguments
about literature as such, or about literature in relation to the world,
to the past, or to modernity. By taking account of Japanese criticism, we acknowledge both the circumstances through which
modern Japanese literature came into being and the necessary limits of any theory or method, East or West.
   A critic like Kobayashi can credibly represent modern Japanese
literature to the world, first of all because he was intimately part of
that literature's configuration. His early work in particular, far
from suppressing other possible ways of reading or interpreting
Japanese literature, openly encourages "multiple designs"—a full
range of critical activity and inter-cultural response. Indeed, Japa-

   19. See note 2 above for claims of "first critic"; for "the god of criticism"
and the Nakagami quote, see Yoshida, pp. 97, 151.

nese critics have much to say about issues that situate Japanese literature at the crossroads of widely shared, contemporary concerns:
the culture of cities, the loss and invention of traditions, ideology
and aesthetics, narration and the nation-state, the dimensions of
the literary self.

In that sense, we do not read Kobayashi to learn how to evaluate
Shiga or Tanizaki correctly, much less, in perpetuation of a truly
fatuous practice, for the Japanese "way" of criticism. Everything
about his early style argues against such passivity and generaliza-
tion. To the degree that he is a critic of consequence in twentieth-
century Japan, he can be of consequence to us. He read other literatures, and not only Japanese literature, as if they closely mattered
to the way he understood himself and his place in the modern
world. He engaged Japanese and non-Japanese writers for the singularity of their expression, for the "marvelous human fact," as he
regularly observed, that no two trees, no two sentences, no two
writers are identical. We might see in Kobayashi aspects of other
critics and of ourselves, yet mistake him for no other.

COMPLETE WORKS

Multiple Designs

(September 1929)

Skepticism may be the beginning of wisdom.
But where wisdom begins, art ends.
André Gide

I

It may be a blessing or a curse, but there is nothing in all the world that is ever once and simply resolved. Language, a gift conferred on humanity along with consciousness—our sole weapon in the advance of our ideas—retains its magical power as of old. There is no language so sublime that it does not beg vulgarity, no language so vulgar that it does not partake of the sublime. Indeed, if language were to dispel its confounding magic over the human heart, it would be but a passing phantom.

It is not my intention here to detail and resolve such questions. I simply wish to address certain facts that our frenetic literary critics have pretended not to see so that they can continue to act frenetically. I regard with great suspicion a literary scene whose emerging critics, as if of professional necessity, are obsessed with one or another ideological design. What happens offstage, behind the scenes as it were, is of greater interest to me than the visible spectacle. And if certain tactics are required to expose our literary situation, I choose to attack from the rear, which seems to me the strategy most suited to any study of the principles of human behavior.

2

Just as poets and novelists inhabit a literary world, so too do literary critics. The poet's desire is to create a poem, a storyteller's to write fiction. Does the literary critic have an analogous wish—to write literary criticism? This is a question rife with paradox.

"How simple," it is said, "to practice criticism by just following one's own taste." But it is just as uncomplicated to practice criticism that follows an ideological yardstick. What is hard is to maintain tastes that are ever vital and alive, and to possess ever living and responsive ideas. People are inclined to think of taste as one thing, ideas another, but to do so is like trying to think of the spirit apart from the body. For example, we can conceive of life on some moon world, but such a life could not become the object of human desire. The miser hoards gold and, in so doing, comes to desire gold. We only truly desire what is possible. This applies as well to the theoretical relations between taste and ideas. How can one possibly possess vital intellectual standards without a sense of taste that is alive? Criticism is an integral act of the spirit. But so long as it seems expedient to split criticism into categories called "taste" and "ideas," then of course we can debate, with considerable care and exactitude, issues of critical method. Still, no matter how conscientious our exploration of a specific critical method may be, it will tell us nothing about why a particular criticism moves us. This is a fact theorists tend to overlook. Consider the case of the man who hopes that he will succeed in love if he studies the rhetoric of the love letter. This person would be a fool if having consummated his love, he attributed the outcome to love letter research. Or else he has consummated something else, but not love.

The evils of subjective or impressionistic criticism have been widely discussed. But all such discussions merely dally around a single principle of decorum or commonsense morality; namely, that "one should not judge others according to one's own likes and dislikes." Perhaps it was neither subjective nor impressionistic criticism that was under attack. Perhaps it was a "criticism that was not criticism." And perhaps the evil of this "criticism that was not criticism" seemed so obvious and intelligible that it provoked no real debate. Still, although I am not at all clear about what literary historians mean when they use mystifying terms like "impressionistic criticism," I am certain about this: when I have before me a sample of impressionistic criticism, say, one of Baudelaire's essays, I am swept away by the movement of its vital sensibility and subtle observations, as if on a ship borne along by the waves. At such moments, captivated by Baudelaire's verbal magic, I see with utter clarity the formal contours neither of his taste nor of his intellectual standards. I see only his dreams that have taken the form of an unparalleled passion. This is justifiably called criticism; it could as well be called a soliloquy. Some have tried variously to separate criticism and self-consciousness. But the magical power of Baudelaire's criticism derives from his awareness that to write criticism is to make oneself conscious. To say that the subject of criticism is the self and the other is to say there is but a single subject, not two. For is not criticism finally the skeptical narration of our dreams?

At this point I would like to address a vulgar expression that presumes itself fashionable: "the universality of criticism." Has there ever been an artist who has stalked this monster, *universality*? Artists without exception seek the particular. It has never been the artist's desire to set forth a truth that holds good in all worlds, in all contexts. It has been the artist's wish only to narrate as completely and faithfully as he can various possible or particular truths. The origin of Goethe's universality lies in his having been a splendid German writer. And the origins of his having been a German writer lie in his having been splendidly personal. With the exception of categorical, transcendental truths, all the proof for various kinds of human truth is to be found amid the human. There can be no basis for a literary criticism cut off from the facticity of human life. The finest criticism is always the most personal. And there is a difference between being merely arbitrary and being personal.

Let us look at the subject from another angle. A person comes into the world embracing various possibilities. He may wish to become a scientist, a soldier, or a novelist, but he can never become other than who he is—a marvelous human fact. To put it another way, a person can discover a variety of truths, but can never entirely possess these truths that are discovered. Multiple truths, in the form of ideas, may reside in the cortex of someone's brain. But there is a single and unalterable truth that courses through the veins of his body. Clouds make rain, and rain makes clouds. The environment makes man, and man makes the environment. Such dialectical statements seem to unite disparate facts and signify the true existence of destiny in the world. But destiny is only meaningful in the context of a person's fate. It signifies the single truth that courses through an individual's body like blood. To speak of an individual's real character and to speak of the artist's creativity is to speak of one and not two separate things. The most profound truths about human nature become part of an artist's work for the single simple and compelling reason that every great artist creates out of himself, and the truths that are revealed in turn construct the character of his work.

Yet no matter how pure the artwork, it is never pure in the sense that scientists speak of "pure water." Art is always replete with multiple shadings, a variety of hues. From out of this plenitude, I can abstract a certain locus of feeling, but this process of abstraction leaves something left over. Wandering through the plenitude of the artwork, I believe I understand the artist's feelings completely, but straightaway, and from a curious angle, the budding part of a new feeling looks back at me. Being thus looked at, I sense the part no longer remaining partial but instantly growing to overwhelm what I thought I had just understood. This wandering through the artwork is analogous to the wandering I do in analysis, trying to grasp my true shape. And so this "I," having experienced the vertigo of self-analysis, hears the bass chords of the author's fate resounding through the profundity of a masterpiece. At this point my reverie comes to an end, and my spirit begins to narrate my language—I am aware of the possibility of my own criticism.

It is not for me to comment on critics who come armed with an array of ideological systems. Perhaps such armor is protective, although it also seems quite cumbersome. And I regard with suspicion the encumbered ideologue's short temper, his inability to be patient and allow the object of criticism to make clear its destiny, its particular characteristics, whatever they may be.

Now to the final complicating paradox. If I call for the emergence of solitary literary critics in our so-called literary world; moreover, if I make it my own life's desire to become wonderfully

solitary, then as a consequence, and in addition to all I have remarked on already at great length, I must give credence to the following statement, at once heroic and absurd: "I must write about
the comedy inherent in every kind of genius, as Balzac wrote his
Human Comedy."

3

Marxist writing. No doubt we find here the ideological design
practiced most widely among contemporary literary critics. Unlike
various other designs that have aesthetic orientations, this one
holds to a political position, and so appears to be the clearest and
least ambiguous of all. But because every design of the spirit is
stamped with a human reality, Marxist writing, too, is susceptible
to a host of controversies.

In ancient Greece the poet was driven out of Plato's *Republic*.
Today he is banished from Marx's *Capital*. For Marx's disciples who
are our present literary critics, this is not an issue of endlessly vac-
illating over what relative value to assign various political or artistic icons. Rather, it is an issue of one passion driving out another.
Yet there is no banishing from this earth passion of any kind. And
what ensures that passion is never banished from the earth is that
there is no place for it to go, nothing beyond this all-sufficient,
however impassive, earth.

I care neither for the phrase "art for the proletariat" nor for the
phrase "art for art's sake." As rhetoric, such expressions are variously colorful, but in the end say nothing substantial. Which is
more difficult: to fight for one's country or for oneself? It sounds
simple to tell someone to make art for the proletariat or to make art
for art's sake, but the artist so instructed is equally vexed.

In the main, ideologies and philosophical systems are not
founded on human consciousness. As Marx noted, "Consciousness
can never be anything but that existence which has been rendered
conscious." An individual's ideology is bound up with his total existence. It is tied to an individual's fate. Because a certain lassitude
is also part of being human, one should find nothing objectionable
about a given writer's indifference to ideology. However, when we
realize that what generates ideology is not in every instance theory

but the forces of human life, then ideology becomes a part of our reality. And although we may not be interested in a particular aspect of reality, we cannot afford to scorn what is real.

If proletarian ideology, to the extent that it finds expression in the finest proletarian literature, does indeed manage to move people, it is because readers are responding to the whole system of relations within the work, and not to its ideas alone. It is because the work is colored by the writer's blood. Those capable of responding to work washed clean of this blood must live according to a cunning theory of human nature whereby "the frivolous heart is moved by frivolities."

Any art of quality possesses a certain reality, like that of someone's glance piercing your heart. If a sign cannot be read as a living structure that moves one toward a passion for reality, then it can be no more than a manual. With a manual, someone can be instructed that by turning right he will reach town. But it cannot make someone who is seated stand up. People do not move because of a manual. They are moved by events. Now a humanly potent ideology is an event. So too is powerful art. And so when they call for using art to advance the proletarian movement, social activists are cleverly using the event of art for their own political interests. They command artists: "Show a heightened consciousness for the social revolution of the proleteriat." But just as there is no one who is not in some sense religious, so too there is no artist who is not of a "heightened consciousness." Without such consciousness, indeed, life would have no direction. Still, no matter how heightened one's consciousness, it always returns to life, because it derives from a perception of life. For the artist, heightened consciousness is but another name for the logic of his artistic creation. And behind this logic can be nothing other than the defining logic of his destiny. The true artist cannot but be faithful to the logic of his particular fate. Should there be any other form of heightened consciousness that involved any less than this, it would be an inert substance having the power neither to poison nor to heal. And what neither poisons nor heals us, we can safely call—unreal.

Another expression—"period consciousness"—recurs in discussions of Marxist writing. Any period has a tone and a coloration distinctive to it. But to the end this remains just a tone or a coloration, not a landscape that we can see clearly. What appears vividly before us is just a structure of various signs given birth by that period's color and tone. A century conveys its most vital myths only when we are caught in the vortex of that century and are acting energetically, unconsciously. I recall the words of Ribot: "The only true knowledge of human interiority comes paradoxically by means of a local anesthetic." It was Baudelaire who at once actualized "self-consciousness," that greatest of nineteenth-century literary passions, and succumbed to it. Indeed this poet was the genius who fulfilled Ribot's admonition. I am not sure if our so-called period consciousness is one of the great twentieth-century literary passions, or if this century will give birth to its own Baudelaire. However, it is plain that the structure of period consciousness will resemble the structure of self-consciousness. It is clear too that period consciousness is of neither greater magnitude nor lesser significance than self-consciousness.

We come now to that antiquarian design: art for art's sake. I do not use the word "antiquarian" indiscriminately. Such a concept would have been incomprehensible to a Greek or a Renaissance artist as descriptive of his attitude toward art. The cult belief that nature imitates art is a perfectly justifiable artistic cult. Thus did Stendhal come to anticipate the appearance of the Sorelian upon writing *The Red and the Black*. But if art does not imitate nature, neither does nature imitate art. Stendahl simply repaid the world what he had borrowed from it. Prior to a belief that his literature would affect the world, he wished for the world to violently affect him. Consequently, "art for art's sake" should not be mistaken as a positive or elated claim that nature imitates art. Rather, it signals a certain cultural debilitation, whereby nature and society have abandoned art. Those who are continually affected by the world cannot abandon it, nor is it their wish to do so. The recluse is not someone who has left the world, but someone whom the world has left behind. Certain centuries possess a myth, a system of belief so alive and animated as to seem almost organic, and to the artist of such a period "art for art's sake" is an absurdity beyond comprehension. Still other centuries are so radically fragmented and broken down that they generate no desire or longing, and so art does not exist.

I cannot tell if our contemporary world possesses a constructive myth or one of decadent ruin. Yet I do not put much faith in Japan's young proletarian writers, whose work is unstained by the blood of human destiny. And I do not trust either our intellectual epicureans, who embrace one cynical dream after another in such rapid succession as to dizzy themselves.

Now as a reader you may wish for dreams that will make your spirit race, or else calm your spirit. But your heart will beat neither faster nor slower. Nature, the physiology of your brain, regulates the speed of your dreams. So long as you disdain such basic facts about human nature, do not complain should an expert ethnographer like Ihara Saikaku come along and write you up under the title "Characteristics and Caricatures of Today's So and So's."

4

It is not for art to reveal a world of truth apart from this world, or again, to depict some other world of beauty. Art is always the place where human passion exists in its clearest symbolic condition. The eternity that some art is alleged to possess is a mere illusion conjured up by aestheticians. Whether they say an object is expressive of "divine inspiration" or "Nature" or "the Great Soul," art cannot in fact rid itself of its human smell. Art is the most human of games, the most paradox-filled expression of what it is to be human. People may claim, for example, that the statues of the Tempyō period possess no individuality, yet it does not follow that what is not individual is not human. Tempyō period craftsmen neither conceived of nor accomplished their work as though it were something isolated from the world. Indeed, they knew nothing of that monster belonging to the modern intellectual called "individuality." We are moved by their craft simply because we feel it to be an expression of the heart.

Those who approach art objectively have just two ways to regard it: as a particular emotion that elicits a particular sign, or as a particular sign that elicits a particular emotion. Here is the reason why a prematurely born "aesthetics," beyond all other disciplines, represents a useless and futile study, at least for the artist. Concept-ridden aestheticians can explain in precise detail what they see as the structure of art, and they can do so because art signifies for them nothing but various artistic sensations. Empirical aestheticians can draw graphs plotting exactly the assorted laws by which art comes into the world, and they can do so because they regard art as just one among a host of expressive techniques to have surfaced over the course of human history. However, for the artist, art is neither a function of sensation nor a function of thought. It is an activity. For the artist, the work is no more than a signpost marking the distance along the way. What is of value is the walking. The artist has no sense of what those who encounter the signposts are going to feel or where they will be led. When the poet writes the final line of a poem, he has simply completed one monument to his ongoing struggle. And if such an inert object as a poetic monument were to become animated and to exist through the ages, it would do so only because of its passage through and its contact with the world of the living.

The element water as "water" has always existed in the world. It is a comparatively recent development to represent water as H_2O. In a similar manner, artists must always create new forms and expressions. What is crucial is not the new form itself, but rather the process of creating the new form. This process remains the dark secret of every artist. I would like to suggest that to the person who embodies this secret, words such as "realism" or "symbolism," circulating in the world like currency or commodities, possess meanings and values beyond their ordinary connotations.

When the gods bestowed Nature on man, it was their wisdom to permit man to know it through naming. Just as we marvel at the discovery of fire, so too should we marvel at the discovery of language. Yet people have come to discard their intuitive sense of what language means, and are drowning in a sea of statements about the wonderful social utility of language. As their reward, some have a quickened feel for social relationships; but in punishment, language now exerts control as a series of designs, each with its own rules and magical formula. At this juncture, the poet who wishes to use the magic of language must first set out from a conscious awareness of its structure.

Consider the example of a child, taught by his mother that the sea is blue. In his attempt to draw a picture of the "sea" around

Shinagawa, the child recognizes that the color of the water which actually appears before him is not blue, or red, or anything else. Should he on impulse throw aside his colored pencils, he would be a genius, but such beings have never existed in the world. Does the child, then, possess a concept such as "The sea is blue"? Of course a child living by Shinagawa Bay would only know the "sea" because of the existence of that bay. For this child, the expression "The sea is blue" exists neither as a concept nor as an empirical object. Now, if this child is to mature and grow in the world, it is imperative that his language become a wanderer within an intermediate space between the conceptual and the empirical.

Throughout life, people remain half-children. What can be said of the adult half? We describe it as being logical. Children become adults by adding to their public practice at language a commonly held sense of logic within language. Yet the poet's activity begins by rejecting this public, shared aspect of language. The full moon hanging in the sky appears to be five inches in diameter, although theory makes evident the falseness of this empirical observation. But the phenomenon of a five-inch moon is not an error. On awakening, people laugh at the absurdity of their dreams, but dream is truth that possesses an imagery distinctive to itself. Flaubert taught Maupassant that "in all the world no two trees or rocks are identical." It was a way of saying: Respect the infinitely rich outward aspects of Nature. But Flaubert's language hints at still another truth; namely, that in all the human world, there is no expression identical to "in all the world no two trees or rocks are identical."

Words, then, are boundlessly rich, each one possessing a particular outward aspect and distinctive connotations. In this respect, lies and falsehood also have their place, as a way to convey what is deceptive and false about life. Perhaps the most startling fact Balzac faced in writing his *Human Comedy* was that the human world was *there,* that it existed while displaying an infinite array of distinct, diverse shapes and forms. That everything in the world is a mystery and that everything in the world is distinct and clear—to Balzac, these were not two separate, contradictory conditions. It would have been impossible for him to see "theory" leaving even the slightest scratch on the skin of Nature. He would have regarded it as being equally absurd to probe for some discovery beneath Nature's skin. For Balzac, wasn't the naked form of that vague ideological design "realism" exposed with utter starkness within the language of Nerval's insanity: "It may be of this world, or it may not be, yet I cannot doubt what I so clearly saw"? Seen in this light, "realism" contains for the artist the basic provisions of his existence, and outlines as well the foundation on which he tries to build his own dream.

Let us proceed a bit further. Whether we are considering a spiritual or a material phenomenon, a humility by which all phenomena are appreciated as being actual and concrete is no doubt the starting point of every great artist. But it does not construct the work itself. The artist's really hard task does not fall within that relatively safe and circumscribed area marked by a "working premise," clear to anyone of an artistic temperament, but outside it, in discovery of the means to construct his dream.

The term "symbolism" is frequently used in contrast to the term "realism." Few terms are as obscure and ambiguous as the aestheticians' use of this term "symbolism." Does any theory exist that makes plain the difference between symbol and metaphor, or between symbol and sign? An aesthetician will explain glibly that a metaphor is the expression of an idea by means of an image, whereas a symbol is the expression of one's impression of an idea by means of an image. Accordingly, Poe's famous *Devil in the Belfry* is neither metaphor nor symbol. Again, aestheticians may speak of a symbol as a sign having an internal imperative that conjoins the existential and the signifying. However, when all is said and done, we can claim little more for a symbol than its status as a superior sign. And only the caprice of the audience labels one sign superior, another inferior.

Following the death of Edgar Allan Poe in 1849, it was Baudelaire who inherited Poe's adventurous project: to banish from poetry all foreign elements and to isolate completely a literary essence. This project reached its pinnacle by way of Mallarmé's hermeticism. People misleadingly called this literary movement "symbolism." It was, rather, a highly intellectualized movement advanced by desperately keen minds who were in fact proposing a certain linguistic materialism. For such writers, the term "symbolism" must have seemed a cheap and listless way to describe their activity.

Reversing the aim of such Romantic composers as Berlioz and Wagner who sought to generate literary effects through sound, the Symbolists tried to infuse writing with musical qualities and in the accumulation of these word-sounds, to produce the effect of music. More precisely, the condition of mind they felt they had captured or could capture moved rhythmically, like music, and could not be expressed in set phrases. It was a sensation that would resonate once the images tied to separate, distinct words had been combined. But music derives from precision-made instruments, and our ears are structured to distinguish sharply between musical sound and random noise. Sound in its purity cannot be compared to the numberless permutations that can occur amid the confusions and the murkiness of language. And so it redounds both to the misfortune and to the glory of these poets that they persisted in believing a musical condition to exist, which could be expressed only through the imagistic form of language.

Readers, often indifferent to the poets' project in this regard, found the effects of the actual poetry to be dim and obscure, and thus rather casually came to use the term "symbolism." Yet the poets themselves were striving to represent as faithfully and directly as possible a state of feeling. Mallarmé's sonnets are the most crystalline forms of his feelings. Some readers regarded them as dim and obscure forms because they were trying to abstract something from the crystal. Mallarmé did not run off to some new land in search of a symbolic existence. He himself became a new country, a new physical presence. Was not the issue facing such a poet in fact one of a most subtle and refined type of realism?

And so the issue of the symbol or the symbolic relates to the effect of the artwork on the audience, and not to the actual practice of a writer. Here I would like to explore why the symbolic value of art, that is, the various effects that the artwork produces, is not terribly significant after all. Of course anyone who reads without affectation and presumption knows this. It requires no special insight.

Fiction does not solve problems. It does create the possibility for their solution. Great fiction always embraces us in waves of surg-

ing thoughts and emotions. But if we so desire, at the point where
these sensations cool and crystallize, we can engage a multiplicity
of problems, as well as the possibilities for their solution. The
greater the surge or intensity a given work possesses, to the degree
that we cannot immediately fathom what sort of problems it presents, the deeper this sense of possibility. What we call the symbolic value of art is just one mode of possibility. Don Quixote wore
the magnificent robes of a symbolic truth called "humanity," and
perhaps even soared off to a starry kingdom. But for me it is enough
to regard how marvelously described, how very full of life, is the
conversation between the jailed Don and Sancho, who had in sorrow followed him. And it is enough to see how the *Divine Comedy*
penetrates into the dream life of Dante, how it reveals both the ten-
derness and the violence of his living soul.

What is called inspiration is something the sincere artist rejects.
His work to the end is a conscious activity. The poet can make poetry only while he is in the persistent act of observing his poetic
work. Still, the sad fact is that most of us regard the actual process
of the poet at work, and the actual effect of the resultant poem, as
separate realities. But how can the poet fully express an artistic effect he is trying to generate? In the middle of his poetic activity,
how can he track the emergence of an unforeseen and unexpected
effect issuing from his own work? Isn't making art like performing
a rope trick of the unconscious, atop a chasm that divides intention
and effect? We speak of the closeness between the genius and the
madman. Does a similar relationship exist between art and absurdity?

Here we encounter, in the most fundamental way, the issue of
the artist's craft or style. Yet who can spy on the secrets of this
world? Even if I were a poet, could I reveal the secrets of my craft?

5

As I was reading an epistemological study of Marxism, I recalled
Gourmont's remark: "Nietzsche was a strange man. He was mad
about common sense." I am not inclined toward such facile sar-
casm and simply wish to make the following observations.

According to the Marxist historical-materialist view that rejects both a materialism attributing consciousness to brain cells and an idealism deriving existence from spirit, "things" in the world are neither whirling spirits nor fixed, determined substances. The historical materialism of Marx, based on a careful and vigorous addition of plain realism to epistemological studies, is a splendid vehicle for a basic understanding of human existence in our time. However, understanding the world in Marxist terms has not the least utility for a person's everyday life. Indeed, common sense cleverly sidesteps Marxism, saying that Marxist insights are too clear, or that the rules governing these insights represent a truth too elegant for mere common sense. Again, from a more detached perspective, should the masses actually comprehend the fundamental laws of Marxism, it would be because these laws are tied to the actual facts of their daily lives, no matter whether they lead a bourgeois or a proletarian existence, or whether existence seems to them a material or a spiritual phenomenon. Those who propagate the notion of the inseparability of modern consciousness and historical materialism are just playing intellectual games. What controls modernity is not things, in the Marxist sense, but what Marx himself explicitly called commodities.

When Balzac looked at the world "as it is," this "as it is" became the method for his own basic understanding of human life. Yet it is plain that those who grasped what Balzac meant only further complicated their actual lives. To go a step further, if we look at this work as Balzac's epistemology, we recognize that the "as it is" style of his *Human Comedy* and the "as it is" human world it means to represent are but a single phenomenon. However, if we look only at the style of the *Human Comedy*, then Balzac's basic rules for human understanding seem like so many dull concepts that have lost their luster. The relations between practice and theory for this individual, Balzac, are surely similar to what they were for the individual, Marx. And there is no difference between them with respect to this fact: that both took as their working premise the representation of the basic characteristics of their age; that both craved nothing beyond the reality which lived and moved before their eyes. Only the personal destinies of Balzac and Marx were different and distinct.

Our Marxist literary critics will scoff at such reasoning for being utterly naive and simpleminded. But isn't the Marxist ideology in their brains neither a praxis informed by theory nor a theory informed by praxis? Isn't it indeed a commodity, displaying all the magic of a commodity? Marxists speak derisively of commodities ruling the world, yet isn't the Marxist design marching through their brains a very marvelous commodity? And Marxism in this guise has the power to make them forget the plain fact that commodities rule the world.

I wish to close by addressing two literary designs not yet touched upon: the writing of the Neo-Perceptionists, and popular writing.

Bourgeois literary theory, proletarian literary theory. I have no idea what such things are, and am not at all disappointed that we cannot depict the shape of such beasts. Marx possessed a certain clear-sightedness, and this allowed him to recognize the collapse of systems of thought in modern times. Yet our so-called Neo-Perceptionist movement emerged precisely because of this collapse, and not because of any recognition or perception about it. This is no positive or active literary movement. It appears in the world as the sign of the debilitation of literature. One might describe Neo-Perceptionist writing as a species of literary formalism, even though it is essentially different from that nineteenth-century formalist movement called Symbolism. The Romantic music that aroused the Symbolists provided them with the most subtle and refined of literary ideas. In this way they came to lament the shabbiness of the ideas in the literature of their day, and when they executed a refinement of those ideas, they realized how equally shabby and impoverished was their language itself.

However, the American music that arouses our Neo-Perceptionists today does not provide them with any sort of literary idea, or anything else that might be loosely described as an ideal. Just as movies require of their audience a heightened visual awareness, so music demands its audience to be all ears. With this in mind, the Neo-Perceptionists decry the existence of ideas in literature as an impoverishment and strive to eradicate them. But compared to their own debilitated ideas, is their writing itself really so powerful?

Popular writing, as I see it, has moved in quite an opposite direction. What we call "popular literature" is less a literature that deals with pleasure than one which is read for pleasure. Were it the intention of popular writers to make literature a form of pleasure, then in today's world, with its surfeit of physical pleasures, surely it is a clumsy method that would first convert raw emotion into a manuscript, and then, by means of writing, try to generate the illusion of real feelings. Rather, popular literature is flourishing today for the simple fact that people cannot be parted from literary illusions. I wish to salute the great exponents of popular literature who amid the confusions of our modern world are passing on the simplest literary idea to have come down through the ages: that of the tale which, like *A Thousand and One Nights*, continues unending from night to night.

. . .

I believe I have passed through the multiple designs of the Japanese literary world today, at least through those that seem important. It was not at all my intention to belittle those designs by suggesting some alternative. It is just that not having too much faith in any one design, I have tried to believe equally in all of them.

NOTE: Kobayashi made minor stylistic revisions in preparing the *zenshū* edition. Also, the original text ended with an allusion to Descartes, which was deleted from the *zenshū* text.

The Anxiety of Modern Literature

(June 1932)

In a recent review, I addressed myself to the work of Kamura Isota in a way many found objectionable. Some voiced their objections in person, others in print. They say that I should not have praised such reactionary writing. How predictable! To label Kamura's work reactionary may be correct, but I have had my fill of such correctness. Indeed, I am instinctively suspicious of anyone who isn't sick of this swill. Think of those tags most beloved of our contemporary critics—"reactionary" and "timely." How filthy they have become, like copper coins, in passing from hand to hand.

Ideology is like a *furoshiki*, useful for stuffing all kinds of things inside. As I write criticism, I am not unmindful of its usefulness. But I sense too the fleeting, ephemeral nature of such utility, the more so as I continue to be impressed by an ever expanding range of high-quality literary work. I've never stepped into a luxury vehicle, plated with theory, and hurtled down an abstract highway called "literature." In fact, I've strewn stones in its path. I just meander along pleasing byways, stopping here and there for a drink. And all I wish from my rare encounters is a heartfelt exchange.

I am neither indifferent to another's darkness, nor do I set out to enlighten anyone. Rather, I always take account of others to educate myself. I have no desire to justify my writing, as if I should be responsible should it appear selfish or unselfish to others. Indeed, such justification would be meaningless, unless it represented obvious resistance to a specific position. Although I've begun this essay by way of a certain justification, in the end I do hope to have written a piece of resistance, however minor, to our literary situation today.

. . .

Some time ago I saw Walter Ruttmann's documentary film, *World Melody*. Tucked into our various corners of Tokyo, scribbling away with our writing brushes, we should welcome the illusionary effects made possible by modern science that permit us to circuit the world in the blink of an eye. Ruttmann's documentary was once described as a species of pure "art film," in other words, as an artistic statement on the beautiful, albeit a new, modern beauty. But what's new one month is obsolete the next. The revolution in cinematic technology raging at the moment has produced a succession of new forms of modern beauty. Why should this be? One explanation is that the masses demand it. But is it really possible that the masses crave modern beauty? What nonsense! I don't believe that people crave such abstractions. It isn't beauty they desire, but a physical sensation. They do not want to learn something, but to forget everything. They seek ways to kill time, burn nervous energy. They do not want to look. They want to be intoxicated.

And so "modern beauty" is just an empty phrase, the invention of film producers or of the film critics who hang about them. If not quite an empty phrase, it is at best jargon coined by critics so driven by a necessity to explain film, a new art form requiring a radical sensory response, that they must toss around such overblown expressions—the beauty of movement, the beauty of speed, the beauty of construction, and so forth. No doubt any number of similar phrases could be used to describe the phenomenon. Meanwhile, haven't we already lost our ability to distinguish between beauty and ugliness, or between sincerity and vanity? Our critical vocabulary has grown meaningless. Yet vibrant images continue to appear before our eyes. How much intellectual labor must we expend before we can take pleasure in them? Our gratitude for the illusionary effects of modern science notwithstanding, shouldn't we be shocked at our insatiable need for ever more detailed and intricate illusions?

Some smile condescendingly on the dreams of the ancients, although no one has that right. It is argued that these days we don't have time for their sort of dreaming. But no one is fully conscious. Perhaps no age prior to our own has been so afflicted by nightmares. Indeed, our nightmares are so numerous and profound that we ridicule the very word "nightmare" as an outmoded figure of speech. Just look at the obvious: our nightmares run so deep that we have grown insensible to them as facts of our existence.

People of old gazed patiently at a landscape and dreamed. When they grew tired of the mountains and rivers existing as ever before their eyes, they willfully transformed these sights into the landscape of their inner feelings. What exists before our eyes today is just this transformed landscape. As did our ancestors, we sit and gaze at this landscape. Curiously, we may sit even more still than they did. The difference is that our chairs move at a hundred yards a second. To be sure, the landscape outside the window remains real and actual, but without recourse to dreaming, what technique will help us endure a reality so changed by the speed of our modern condition? There is no such technique, and so we continue dreaming. We alight from a plane only to take a car. There is no interval whatsoever to awaken from the dream. As for the welter of bizarre images needed to weave our dreams: science uses them to construct the environment around us, without our conscious intervention. And because of science, we have lost the patience, courage, and ease to fashion our own dreams.

. . .

Of course the miracle of the machine, created by science, presupposes the miracle of theory that underlies it. Given our enlightened awareness of the galaxy, we were poised to see that the movement of electrons bears a close resemblance to planetary movement. It also became clear that maximum entropy is analogous to the process of dying. Light beams, formerly thought to overcome darkness, were transformed into substances with specific weight. In turn, we recognized not only that light surrounds us even on a dark night, but that it suffuses our spirit world and constructs it. Once the movement of each atom was seen to wave unsteadily, time and space, as pure concepts, lost all significance. To the amateur who only peeks in on science, such crucial theorems seem like the stuff of dreams. And we would be less than honest were we not to express genuine wonder before all that modern science has accomplished.

Nothing remains fixed and certain. In the human sciences today, new facts are accorded the greatest significance. To our eyes, exhausted in pursuit of these new facts, the color of things multiplies, outlines blur—nothing remains fixed and certain. If we can steal a bit of time and close our eyes in quiet contemplation, we find that waves of new ideas generate an epistemological crisis. Paradox becomes our way of thinking. In our time, any intellectual who claims to be oblivious to paradox is either a fool or a liar.

We go into the streets full of anxiety. Nothing exists out there that we can call "the city" or "society" with any certainty. Strangely, each and every thing necessary for a city or a society lies right before our eyes: the railway station, the post office, buildings, and factories. But we have no stable belief in what exists behind them, the strings that make them run. And when we dive into a bar, driven by a purposeless urge to consume something, aren't we even suspicious of the money that pops from our wallets?

You young writers, you masochists who, secure in your own world, go fishing for a "guiding principle" to be found in some critic's theory—don't waste your time asking me what you should do. There are others prepared to answer such a question. You would do better to get the opinion of those social theorists who have reconfigured the modern world as if it were a laboratory and are consumed in their intricate calculations, gauging human beings like mice.

. . .

Of late the word "robot" has become fashionable. I read in the newspaper of a robot who climbed a chimney. And I have actually seen a robot, equipped with a lighted belly button and a phonograph built into its torso, dancing with a showgirl. But robots were born with the invention of the steam engine and were endowed with "intelligence" about the time radium was discovered. Nature and man no longer confront each other. Standing between them is the machine. What rules over man are not the laws of nature, but mechanical laws. They are the artificial, almost fantastical laws of a robot turning to rust. Moreover, we presume to follow these tyrannical laws with a physiological apparatus that has lasted without modification for over 100,000 years.

The Classical school sought the parameters of its artistic production in the limpid form of a nature not subject to analysis, as well as in the movements of a body not yet differentiated from mind. With the Romantics, there was a shift toward an investigation of the apparatus of feeling, of the passions. Moreover, the Romantics deliberately privileged dreams, ridiculing the utilitarianism of the social world while never losing sight of the special claims of nature. In time, utilitarianism, which had maintained its proximity to social forms and conventions, burst forth as positivism. At this juncture, writers who were no longer able to dream joined hands with a former enemy. Naturalism thus revealed its pathetic face, as it accommodated itself to the deterministic theories of the enemy. Pater understood this. He recognized the tragedy of modern literature, wherein fate no longer exists outside humanity but within, as an intricate web spun inside the brain, perceived in solitude by each individual. Some writers tried to escape from this web and once again spin their dreams in the world, but too late. The enemy had spun a dream of exceeding complexity traveling at nearly the speed of light. With no recourse, writers again joined hands with a smug enemy. In fact, as they later realized, fantasy and reality were joined inside their own heads. "Pathetic" was no longer the right word to describe the tragic condition they now faced. Anxiety had arrived. Anxiety—the greatest drama on stage within the modern spirit.

. . .

The truly unfortunate are not those who feel unfortunate but those who have grown accustomed to such feelings. The human mind is ruled by a strange dialectics of nature. Once people have experienced extreme anxiety, they feel that they cannot live without it. Anxiety may not become their god, but it becomes at least their prop. In the past, anxiety was thought to be an illness of the spirit, whereas in our time it represents a normal condition. These days, people talk incessantly. They rattle on—anxious over this, anxious over that—but strangely their voices register not the slightest trace of fear. Self-advertisement is ablaze precisely when someone has lost himself. So bizarre are the illusions ruling our literary world today that even those who pay lip service to dialectical theory are unable to comprehend the simple dialectics of modern anxiety.

My following remarks are not intended for our older or middle-aged writers and critics, who have turned away and indiscriminately despise all theory. I don't expect them to write literary reviews as difficult and complex as those of their younger counterparts. But I do want to address intellectuals of my own generation, regardless of ideological allegiance, who have been raised in a similar environment and have received the same type of education.

What follows has struck me recently, if for reasons that remain unclear. I think that among our young writers, thought has become but a pretext or an excuse for action. As a result, it is hard to grasp the truly human dimensions of thought itself. Language can be reductively simple, while the facts of reality are complex. A capacity for self-deception spreads its net over the world of our passions, over every corner of our feelings, over our affections and hatreds, to the very ends of our sensibility. In this way, no matter how carefully society is examined, how many books are read, or how many political actions are simulated, we never cast off self-deception. And so language and reality remain unreconciled. For such a reconciliation to occur we need to look back and examine the self. My own limited experience instructs me that my mistakes and misperceptions came not from an excess of feeling but from an excess of thinking, or from an ideology that took no account of the self and others. In other words, the obstacle to seeing the true shape of things is not feeling as such, but feeling under the control of ideology. Never has there been a literature like the "new literature" of our day, which shamelessly parades every vanity and perversity of the youthful heart. Never has there been a time when theory, rooted in self-forgetfulness and preoccupied with social uneasiness, so held sway.

For example, there is an ideology called "individualism," and there is one called "anti-individualism." Aren't they both the projections of drowning men who are grasping at straws? Should we be grateful to a world that lets us swim, so long as we grasp such a straw? But the world is not so cruel a place as it is often made out to be. One attacks another for being an "individualist," although the attack is unwarranted because the person attacked does not possess individuality in the first place. Our contemporary literary battles present spectacles of just this kind. If you take these things seriously, you deserve whatever you get.

By my estimate, nine out of ten of our "new writers" are ungrounded in the literature of this country. Older writers criticize them for their glorification of foreign writing, but they are also ignorant of much of the best European work of the past 100 years. Least of all do they reveal any scrutiny or knowledge of themselves. No one undertakes a serious self-questioning. But when one's own past is rendered meaningless, can any meaning be discovered in people of a more remote past? What insights can one possibly bring to bear on the present? What do our writers have in front of them but a blank sheet of manuscript paper, a pen, and an assortment of the latest literary magazines? And they possess merely the vacuous impulse to probe somebody else's theory or method. Why don't they begin by questioning themselves? Why do they clamor for clarity and certainty about every aspect of human nature, when they are young and have yet to expend their own intellectual efforts? Isn't it a truly odd spectacle to witness their proficiency in all the latest methods, when at their age they can hardly comprehend what it means to be human? And so the most prophetic ideologies proliferate by way of the clumsiest expressions.

. . .

The "intellectual" type seems to be in fashion. But only provisionally can we call it fashionable. Although a new term—the intellectual—has been coined, not a single writer has yet provided a powerful realization of this intellectual type in a story or novel. I am an intellectual myself, and hope to live out my allotted time as one of this unfortunate species.

The *bundan* that uses "the intellectual" as a synonym for "weak-willed and naive" is itself totally composed of intellectuals. I have before me an essay composed by a certain college student, Mr. X, who pompously claims that someone's proletarian novel is unacceptable because of its "intellectual flavor." Turning to the editor's postscript, we are enjoined to appreciate the "subtle astringency" of Mr. X's essay style. This type of farce is a sign of our times.

In an earlier generation, writers frequently depicted morally bankrupt characters. I recall encountering such characters in fiction, who seemed tragic to me. But I no longer have such feelings. What I encounter today is a senseless vacillation or a vague anxiety expressed by our intellectual writers who, relinquishing the effort to explore themselves, ignoring their own flesh and blood in feverish pursuit of new theories, have turned their methodologies into wooden idols. Even when they try to be honest about their present dilemma, they can do little more than give us the old, morally bankrupt character. As writers, have you been reduced to this, after all? Are your own lives not sufficient material for your writing?

How did intellectual writers before our age deal with the bankrupt character? What touch did they use? They did not so much represent a morally bankrupt character as lyricize him. It was a natural song of self-loathing. Now, self-loathing is one way to indulge the self. It is the most paradoxical form of self-intoxication. Self-loathing lurked behind their songs. Of course the social environment that surrounded them was not as bewildering as our own. It still permitted writers the full display of a literary temperament. They claimed to be oppressed, but by what? Perhaps it was the positivism of the common people they despised, and which offended their refined sensibilities. And when their contempt for the common people joined with habits of self-cultivation inherited from the Naturalists and became inbred, it resulted in odes to the morally bankrupt character. Their despair, as voiced by such characters, was the product of a poetic temperament. A prose spirit would not have gotten itself so involved.

Akutagawa is the most poignant example of those wounded by such poetic despair. Many critics argue that Akutagawa is the figure who most singularly embodied the fate of the modern intellectual. I believe they are mistaken. This rare talent was in the end just an essayist who left behind fine, impressionistic writings, but could not portray a single human character. I even question whether his insights into human nature were superior to those of several, far less famous Naturalists.

When we examine how our writers greeted Dostoevsky, the look in their eyes when he was first imported to this country, we see to what extent our novelists of a generation ago were really poets. In his youth, Dostoevsky had exhaustive personal experience of the morally bankrupt character, so that when he came to depict such a character in his novels, he could do so as a confirmed realist. Every type of morally bankrupt character in Dostoevsky's work is constructed by a powerful imaginative force—not fantasy—and strides with vigor across the fictional stage. But our poets who called themselves novelists, grasping mentally the mere concept of a "bankrupt character" without ever having witnessed this concept come to life in human action, just stared vacantly upon the Dostoevsky spectacle. Because they had no direct way to engage him, they thought him to be unnatural, perverse. His greatest novels were read once, but not re-read. When we were students, our generation read Dostoevsky ecstatically, then put him aside.

But now, truly, the time has come when we must engage Dostoevsky. We are surrounded by the "possessed." A procession of small, bankrupt characters has gone forth from the heads of earlier writers, and is now walking the streets. It is the responsibility of our novelists today to discover their character types among them. It will do no good to stare at reality, or to conduct research from a detached perspective. Nor will it do any good abruptly to cancel such objectivity, and to depict every manager, say, as being bespectacled, fat, and lazy.

. . .

In his last years, Akutagawa Ryūnosuke was consumed by the strife between a poetic and a prose spirit. More than any writer of his generation, he thought clearly about this problem, although his literary struggles were exceedingly neurotic, and his personal hardships were of a similarly pathological nature. However, with the emergence of proletarian literature (or perhaps better, with the wish for a proletarian literature), the problem seemed to be suddenly and forcibly resolved. A pure prose spirit that cast not the slightest glance in the direction of the lyric suddenly asserted itself, albeit within a tradition of fiction that suffered from a deficiency of prose-spiritedness. This is the greatest single gift the proletarian literary movement has bestowed on Japanese letters to date. However, because the matter is so very Japanese, both proletarian novelists and critics have lost sight of its significance.

The source of our current disorder is to be found here as well. A prose spirit that sets out to construct "the novel"—which as far as possible would not fall prey to emotions, remaining faithful instead to the dialectics of nature; which would be simple and direct, avoiding lyricism and beauty—such a prose spirit is something our writers never achieved through their own struggles. Rather, it became an ideology that served as an excuse for action by writers who felt oppressed by society. Perhaps this ideology is a correct one, but who can take pride in embracing an ideology because it is correct? So long as they were convinced that they possessed a correct ideology, writers made no patient effort to give it human form. And so they abandoned every method that might have put flesh on this spirit. In fact, they gave up being writers, and now speak as theorists or politicians instead, proclaiming that "for me, literature works differently." But can they continue to say that they love literature?

And so discussions around the topic "politics and literature" grew rampant. The extreme contentiousness of the past several years over literary and political values, seems finally to have settled on the notion of the dialectical unity of literature and politics. Indeed, it appears of late that this term "dialectical" is one of truly extraordinary range and utility.

But what does it mean to speak of the "dialectical unity" of literature and politics? Does it mean that writers must show up at committee meetings seven times a day? Does it mean writing about subjects distinctly foreign from oneself, having left behind (or "liquidated," to use the term now in vogue) the environment where one was raised, one's education, even one's talent? Does it mean that the comrade who suffered in isolation from the world for two years, cannot write the novel he conceived in isolation? If the answer is "no, he cannot write it, at least given the urgency of these times," then the mendacity of our situation becomes doubly clear.

I have no faith in politicians or in political arrangements. Still, I have a sense of ethics as it applies to the political. I do not ridicule in the least the passion of young readers. Yet I know something about the vanity of a youthful reliance on ideology, about the deceptiveness of concepts that arouse youth. This deceptiveness mixes even with the tears you shed upon parting from a comrade, or upon his death. From your work I already know how jaundiced is your view of human nature, how cynically you regard the subject of love. And from life experience, I know something about your loves and about your bizarre conjugal struggles. Even as you raise the banner of socialism, you reveal contempt for humanity. This I call madness.

. . .

Before all else, our literature today propagates theory, attitude, position. In consequence, debates take place between competing ideological designs. But no one says a word about the sharpness or dullness of a given design, about its capacity to expose the structure and stuff of reality. What writers most need, especially today, is solitude and independence. In this hour, when vacuous theories threaten to displace the writer or to overshadow the writer's presence, each writer should work tirelessly to discover his own destiny, his own possibility, his own desire. As Valéry once said: "All too often, and quite carelessly, our own thoughts come to us through the expressions of others."

NOTE: Minor, stylistic corrections (*ga* replaces *da ga; dewa* is dropped at sentence beginnings, etc.) were made by Kobayashi for the *zenshū* edition. The last line of the original was also dropped. It read: "The sickness of our era, or if that sounds too strong, the purest expression of our era's sickness, is to be found here."

Literature of the Lost Home

(May 1933)

It might be said that in Japan today a literature read by adults or by old people scarcely exists. Our politicians are taken to task for their lack of literary sophistication, or for being oblivious to what is happening in the literary world, but does the blame not lie with the literati themselves? People are not necessarily cool or indifferent to literary matters. . . . Still, it is true that adult taste runs mostly toward the Chinese classics, or else toward certain Japanese classics, though certainly not toward modern writing. Modern Japanese literature, especially what is known as "pure literature," is read by young people, that is, by a certain "literary youth" between the ages of eighteen and thirty, or to stretch the point, by writers only, or else aspiring writers. . . . Our so-called *bundan* is in fact a special world populated almost entirely by like-minded youth, and this situation has not changed since the days of Naturalism. Although a proletarian writer might be expected to have an interest in political institutions or in social conditions, once he becomes a member of the literary world, and is absorbed in writing monthly review columns, his readership narrows to that limited sphere which is the focus of pure literature itself. Few can claim to have avid readers scattered widely throughout the population, among farmers and workers, for example. Of all our arts, literature alone is trapped inside this narrow and cramped universe. Of course it is well known that Japanese music and painting, not to mention the theater, have always maintained a broad-based and devoted patronage. Popular literature, too, as if in compensation for having been exiled from the monthly reviews of the literati, seems to attract a circle of readers drawn from every sector of the society. Yet even here, the overwhelming majority of its fans are doubtless men and women under thirty. I am approaching fifty and can feel only sadness, knowing that the likely readers of my work will be youth. And putting myself in the position of the adult reader, who claims there is nothing he can bear to read beyond the classics, I must acknowledge that our modern literature is somehow defective. For only that writing which one has leisurely perused by the hearth, which has offered consolation and a lifetime of untiring companionship—only such writing can be called true literature.

As I was reading Tanizaki Jun'ichirō's essay "On Art" (in the April issue of *Kaizō*), I encountered the above passage, and fell to brooding about it. I did not brood with any thought to refute Tanizaki, or with any sense that I could resolve his dilemma. Mine was the useless brooding of a man, in Tanizaki's words, "trapped inside a narrow and cramped universe," and my feelings turned heavy and gloomy.

Reading over both parts of the "On Art" series, it occurred to me that although Tanizaki's style was measured, his conviction was intense. If in formal terms the writing seemed obscure, what the author wanted to say was nevertheless unmistakably clear. Such intense conviction and unequivocal opinion, were we to look for a counterpart, might be found in an address given at Kudan Nōgaku Hall by George Bernard Shaw, whom Tanizaki himself has dubbed the "boyish-grandpa": "Ladies and gentlemen, humanity is hopeless! Many of those who are artists, however bad, declare that they cultivate art for the sake of humanity. This is not so. Let us leave to the Philistines of the outside world the pretense that everything they do for us is for the good of humanity."

Shaw's words in themselves are of no special interest. In our day it is not at all strange that a writer's passion would assume a certain peevish, perverse expression. Yet in the power and integrity of the sentiments Tanizaki himself expresses, which are founded on that author's lifelong experience, something else is at work, something hard to fathom, which provokes in us readers a heavy, gloomy feeling. Tanizaki concludes his essay by remarking that "young people who laugh at my perversity will perhaps come around to my way of thinking when they reach my age." Although at my present age I have yet to "come around," I wonder—Has Tanizaki said anything to invite my ridicule?

Whenever someone refers to me as an *Edokko*, I grimace. This is because a rather considerable distance separates what others mean by this expression and what I take it to mean. Most people of my generation who were born in Tokyo know very well how bizarre it is to claim this city as a birthplace. Recourse to an expression like *Edokko* is wholly unsuitable. People like myself feel their situation will not be understood by outsiders. Even among those born in Tokyo, there is a sense of difficulty in expressing one's feelings to anyone even slightly older.

I have neither thought of myself as an *Edokko*, nor do I possess what are known as "Edo tastes," although perhaps unconsciously I harbor traces of an *Edokko* temperament. This is fine with me. I have never lamented the situation. Still, I have never lived without even stranger feelings of incomprehension. "Born in Tokyo"—I cannot fathom what that really means. Mine is an unsettled feeling that I have no home. It should be recognized that this is not in the least a romantic feeling, although it may be harder to see that there is nothing realistic about it.

Once I was traveling from Kyoto with Takii Kōsaku. As our train emerged from one tunnel, the mountain roads suddenly flashing into sight, he gazed up and heaved a deep sigh. I was struck by this. Listening to him then describe the fullness of his heart, how gazing upon such mountain roads a stream of childhood memories came welling up within him, I keenly felt that the "country" exists beyond my comprehension. It is not so much that I do not know the country as I do not understand the notion of a "birthplace," or a "first home," or a "second home"—indeed, what home of any kind in fact is. Where there is no memory, there is no home. If a person does not possess powerful memories, created from an accumulation of hard and fast images that a hard and fast environment provides, he will not know that sense of well-being which brims over in the word *kokyō*. No matter where I search within myself for such a feeling, I do not find it. Looking back, I see that from an early age my feelings were distorted by an endless series of changes occurring too fast. Never was there sufficient time to nurture the sources of a powerful and enduring memory, attached to the concrete and the particular. I had memories but they possessed no actuality, no substance. I even felt they were somehow unreal.

Putting aside this rather exaggerated example, we all on occasion recall something our mother might have told us about her own childhood. Just a simple story, nothing special or inspiring, and yet for that very reason a strong and unwavering sentiment courses through it. A story of such commonplace memories contains the precondition for fiction. And so I am envious, because no matter how I try, this is something I cannot replicate. Without embellishment, or if that sounds too crass, without a device allowing a subjective response—a point of view or a critical perspective—I feel my memories would have no unifying structure, even as I realize that however necessary, the use of such devices is somehow unnatural.

Once it occurred to me that mine was a spirit without a home, I found evidence for it everywhere. It is especially instructive to record certain extreme experiences. I enjoy walking and often go off to the mountains, being someone who takes pleasure in remote, even dangerous places. Of late I have come to realize how odd such behavior is. To go off for inspiration to the beauty of Nature may seem to be a perfectly natural activity, but on reflection we must admit that it is just another manifestation of our quotidian intellectual unease. It is not at all a matter as straightforward and reasonable and innocent as "loving nature." I have grown increasingly skeptical about the existence of anything concrete and actual behind my being moved by the beauty of Nature. Looking closer, I see much in common between intoxication by the beauty of a mountain, and intoxication by the beauty of an abstract idea. I feel as though I am looking upon two aspects of a spirit that has lost its home. Consequently, I am not heartened by the recent craze for mountain climbing. And I feel all the more uneasy as the number of afflicted climbers rises each year.

On reflection, I know that my life has been lacking in concrete substance. I do not easily recognize within myself or in the world around me people whose feet are planted firmly on the ground, or who have the features of social beings. I can more easily recognize the face of that abstraction called the "city person," who might have been born anywhere, than a Tokyoite born in the city of To-kyo. No doubt a meditation on the various components of this ab-straction may produce a certain type of literature, although it will be deficient in real substance. The spirit in exhaustion takes flight from society and is moved by the curiously abstract longing to commingle with Nature. It may well be that a world of actual sub-stance is to be found in the beauty of Nature isolated from society, yet there is no reason to believe any real writing will come of it.

In his essay, Mr. Tanizaki referred to a "literature that will find a home for the spirit." Of course for me this is not a mere literary is-sue, since it is not at all clear that I have any real and actual home.

. . .

The other day, rereading Dostoevsky's *Raw Youth* in the Yone-kawa Masao translation, I was struck by several things that had not occurred to me when I first read this book. In particular, I sensed the importance of the title chosen by the author. Illuminating the world seen by a single youth through the language of a single youth, the author revealed all the attributes of youth in general: its beauty and ugliness, hypersensitivity and insensibility, madness and pas-sion and absurdity; in short, its authentic shape. I was left with an almost unbearably strong feeling that it is incorrect to call young people "youth." They are rather a species of animal that must be called by some other name. It struck me too that Dostoevsky's youth is no stranger—a youth whose mind is in turmoil because of Western ideas and who, in the midst of this intellectual agitation, has utterly lost his home. How very closely he resembles us. In-deed, I repeatedly ran into scenes that made me feel the author was describing me, that he had me firmly in his grasp.

"Our so-called *bundan* is in fact a special world populated al-most entirely by like-minded literary youth," Tanizaki writes, "and this situation has not changed since the days of Naturalism." How-ever, the role of youth in literature seems to me to have grown steadily more blatant. In the days of Naturalism, issues of social or-der or social chaos were not so clearly pressing as they are today. As a consequence, we are overwhelmed and prone to sacrifice our re-flective spirit for the sake of dreams about the future, our ideas for the sake of action, our feelings for the sake of ideas, facts for the sake of theories, the ordinary for the sake of adventure. In short, we might say that as society has assumed a youthful character, it has cheapened the value of a mature spirit. It is then perfectly natural that the *bundan* too should become increasingly a special world of youth, although this is not reason enough to question the value of the literature it produces. Still, I believe that formerly literature brought as many benefits to society as it induced any evil. Given our situation today, I can only feel that the evil, by degrees, is spreading.

It cannot be claimed that mature adults necessarily have no interest in literature about youth. For example, *The Sorrows of Young Werther* is a type of "youth writing," yet it has been able to attract great numbers of people. It is not, then, just a matter of recent Japanese literature being literature by and for youth. Rather, ours is a youth literature that has lost its youth. And whatever its intentions may have been, in practice is it not the distinctive trait of such literature to be fundamentally conceptual and abstract, and, at least since turn-of-the-century Naturalism, to come more and more to lack a taste for reality? Of course we should not always overlook literary motives or intentions and regard only practice or results. But it is in the practice of such "youth writing" that we are able to discover not only these current, vigorously debated issues regarding society and economics, but also the peculiar context and inevitable fate of the literary youth of our nation, who feel the urgent sway of Western models and influence, and who have lost a sense of tradition.

Popular writers have emerged recently to attack the narrowness of "artful" literary fiction, proclaiming its demise. However, these popular novels also exhibit a spectacle unique to our country. The readership of our literary fiction may be young, but it takes a certain literary sophistication to understand such work, and there are a number of very fine books that could not be fully appreciated were they to be read by adults, sophisticated only in worldly affairs. Of course I cannot imagine mature adults reading the alternative: modern popular fiction. Adults are not about to read a story, however interestingly written, about what they already know, and that reveals no further discoveries. And so they turn to historical romances, *magemono*. Surely it is not so elsewhere, but in our country conditions are such that most popular writing relies not on contemporary incidents but on historical tales for its contact with an audience of adult readers.

This becomes all the clearer if we turn to film. From the outset our film masterpieces were done in the old style, on historical themes. The fine actors and directors all tended in that direction. In comparison to literature, film is a far more immediate artistic medium, and so one need hardly argue the point that the average fan would likely wish his masterpieces to be based on contemporary events. In Japan a contrary situation exists, although we must admit that, if not for Japanese films, we would not recognize so clearly the true strangeness of our cultural condition.

Historical romances and *chambara* movies exert a profound influence over the masses. Although this peculiar phenomenon may not be long-lived, it cannot be argued that it will easily pass away. Its roots are quite strong. Some suggest that in a period of social collapse, when no definite or stabilizing ideas are in force, people have a renewed desire for sensual stimulation or excitement. Still, I do not feel this alone can explain the popularity of such fare. If that were the only reason, these popular entertainments would have no hope of such success. Farfetched subjects and convoluted plots alone would not spark the interest of the masses, no matter how culturally naive they may be. I believe that the hearts of the masses are captured almost involuntarily along a slower but surer path. Their interest turns on the capacity of a film to make them unconsciously surrender to a stream of real emotions. This stream flows through our *chambara* movies, though not through our *gendaimono*—movies about modern life.

I often go to the movies with my mother. Of course her preference is the period film, as she finds nothing of interest in *gendaimono*. Once I took her to see the Western film *Morocco*. It occurred to me that this was quite futile, but to my surprise she was greatly moved by it. She has since cultivated a taste for Western movies. Even my old mother, then, has been overwhelmed by the complications and confusions of our modern Japanese art forms and has turned away.

Morocco has been called a modern masterpiece, but its content is in fact quite shallow, and in this respect there are a number of our *gendaimono* that address more serious concerns. However, *Mo-*

rocco has a certain style that our films about modern life cannot match. It possesses a wholly captivating charm that leaves no room for discussion about its plot meaning this or that. And what is most lacking in our *gendaimono*, as well as in our current popular fiction, is just this inexplicable style. Were we to inquire why such entertainment, utterly lacking in such style, nevertheless has fans to see it or to read it, we might find the reason is that the majority are satisfied simply with the plot. Being young, of an age when the world is seen through movies and life is known through fiction, this audience does not question whether a given work lets flow a stream of real emotions so compelling as to overpower a mere plot. Only when such youths reach maturity will the plot seem silly to them, and all but unconsciously will they begin to look for the kind of style that might conceal the silliness.

In film, this demand is presently met by period pieces or by Western movies; in literature, by popular renditions of historical adventure. The manners and mores that appear in *chambara* movies and in *magemono* fiction already seem as distant and removed from us as the manners and mores depicted in Western films. Still, the psychology and emotional temperament expressed in such works seem perfectly in harmony with the social scenery of that time. And the expression of such human feelings, free of contradiction, possesses an unimaginably powerful charm and fascination. This style elicits a sense of intimacy, so that we feel closer to the Moroccan desert we have never seen than to the landscape of Ginza before our eyes.

Some speak of the modern world as one beset by a common, universal social crisis, although I can only feel that contemporary Japanese society is collapsing in a quite distinctive way. Obviously, our modern literature (for all practical purposes we might substitute "Western" for "modern") would never have emerged without the influence of the West. But what is crucial is that we have grown so accustomed to this Western influence that we can no longer distinguish what is under the force of this influence from what is not. Can we possibly imagine the profound emotion and wonder that Futabatei's *Ukigumo* (Floating cloud) or [Mori] Ōgai's *Sokkyō shijin* (Improvisation) aroused in the youth of their day, we who came of literary age when translations were so numerous that they could not all be read? Can we fear that anything remains to be taken away, we who have lost a feel for what is characteristic of the country of our birth, who have lost our cultural singularity? Is it any consolation to think that those writers of a preceding generation, for whom the struggle between East and West figured crucially in their artistic activity, failed to lose what we have succeeded in losing?

It is a fact that ours is a literature of the lost home, that we are young people who have lost our youthful innocence. Yet we have something to redeem our loss. We have finally become able, without prejudice or distortion, to understand what is at the core of Western writing. With us Western literature has begun to be presented fairly and accurately. At this juncture, it is indeed pointless to call out for the "Japanese spirit" or the "Eastern spirit." Look wherever we might, such things will not be found. Or what might be found would prove hardly worth the search. And so Mr. Tanizaki's notion that we must "return to the classics" will not readily be embraced and passed on. It speaks simply to the fact that Tanizaki himself has chosen a certain path and matured in a certain direction. History seems always and inexorably to destroy tradition. And individuals, as they mature, seem always and inexorably to move toward its true discovery.

NOTE: The zenshū text is identical to the original publication except for the last line, which was dropped. It read: "With the passing of time, history reveals in clearer outline to the writer certain objective facts, and presses on him a structure that he can in no way evade. And, as the writer matures, his character becomes more and more concrete and distinctive, and paradoxically becomes part of the content of the [historical] structure that presses upon him."

Chaos in the Literary World

(January 1934)

1. On Criticism

I thought of calling this piece "On the Literary Revival" but decided against it. Had I used such a title, surely someone would have piped up, absurdly but with great conviction, that "according to Kobayashi Hideo, literature has revived." Elsewhere, already, one smug critic has written: "Although I am quite dubious about the outcome, it would seem that voices calling for a rebirth of pure literature are rising, along with those who rejoice at the expected coming of the glorious day of literary revival." Stop posing, I want to tell this critic. Who, after all, has been calling for a rebirth of pure literature? Where, precisely, are the writers who are revealing their joy over a literary revival? Does a single critic exist who has written an essay heralding the dawn of this revival?

I am not suggesting that we try to get hold of the true shape of this phantom revival. I am saying that we should not create phantoms unnecessarily. Whether they are in sympathy with or scorn a revival, why don't critics start with plain, simple facts, such as the recent appearance of two or three more literary magazines? Who could possibly be impressed, not by such facts, but instead by the "analysis" of a phantom, built by a mob of spectators, that is made out to be either the vestige of some past or the sign of some present crisis? We have arrived at the height of absurdity when we start to suspect that this phantom is not the construction of a whole mob, but an invention made by a lone critic for his convenience. How warped indeed are the conditions of our criticism!

Each year, come December, the review sections of our newspapers and magazines present us with the seasonal spectacle of critic-poseurs. "Oh my," such critics exclaim, "how many wonderful things happened this year." What lies. Moreover, the makers of these claims never introduce us to literary issues of real importance and complexity. Indeed, isn't it the case that far from introducing us to such problems, they have instead killed them off?

It is characteristic of the anxiety of our age that one after another, at complete random, problems of all kinds should be spread before us. Again, it is characteristic of these problems that they should be presented in a form vulnerable to attack and destruction. Now it does not take much effort to twist or to kill. A given problem emerges, and everyone rushes toward it and begins to resolve it. And so something is being resolved, but we should observe that it never existed as a proper, formal problem in the first place. We have resolutions to problems, then, that have yet to take shape. This is not wordplay on my part, but a faithful account of a situation that is truly strange.

There was the recent controversy over "the impotence of criticism." I know it well because I was made out to be a perpetrator of this condition. Charges against my useless, impotent criticism encircled an impressionistic piece I wrote in the August issue of *Kaizō*, titled "On Criticism." Now it had been my intention there to underscore the power and potency of criticism. But my manner of expression was admittedly subjective and somewhat perverse. Still, I did manage to express the following positive conviction: "Just as great writers are not necessarily aware of the methods by which they write, so too are distinguished critics unaware of the range of paradox contained within their critical methods. I long to see the emergence of a great critic whose strong critical practice will overcome the entanglements of method." Now for whatever reason, what I was saying here was misunderstood. As a matter of fact, I am not upset at the misunderstanding itself. Something even more lamentable is at stake. For isn't it shameful that any problem would be thought "resolved" by my admittedly slight essay?

No matter how orderly its structure, any problem as such will eventually die. No matter how modest its scale, any problem at the moment of its inception lives. If there is a vital issue to begin with, then it will be dispersed through every sentence that I write. Indeed, I consciously infuse it into my writing. But who will allow me to nurture this vitality as my own? Who will permit it to expand, deepen, and itself become a focus of critical discussion? As a critic, I should not have to waste my time worrying about whether my criticism will be judged "potent" or not.

Critics today pursue novelties, but do not seek true vitality. They are fond of building one new problem after another, but are not inclined to give new forms of expression to a given problem. They are fond of resolving random issues in the same way, but are not inclined to resolve each one in a new and distinctive way. This is because it is far more difficult to discern what constitutes the new or the old about a given problem than to address ready-made "new problems" or "old problems." The tendency to drift toward increasingly expedient critical methods is a strong inertial force within our *bundan*. It is an illness easily transmitted to our critics. For any lazy critic who has climbed aboard this inertia, solving problems seems far less troublesome than introducing them properly. Indeed, we can say that only those problems are being introduced that have already been resolved. Many critics can only resolve problems that are introduced in this manner. This I do not call the real work of the critical spirit. Yet owing to such well-built solutions, how many really vital questions have been buried? How many intricate possibilities within a given problem have been ruled out at the halfway point? In this way, time and again, vital literary issues have become grist for a desiccated *bundan*. And so we hear them exclaim: "How many wonderful things happened this year." They are the voices of fools, or demons.

Yazaki Dan, in a critique of my work, writes that my spirit is one which abhors judgments. But does Yazaki know what a "spirit which abhors judgments" really is? Can he in good conscience say that he knows it? His argument makes no sense. And so I feel under no obligation, based on the connotations of his critical vocabulary, to accept his fashionable notion about my "spirit which abhors judgments."

I regard all things, not just criticism, skeptically. But I take no pleasure in my skepticism. In fact, I do not have the spiritual leisure to enjoy it. I am possessed only by an arrogant wish to pursue each and every possibility of which my spirit is capable. Indeed, it is this wish alone that drives my spirit toward skepticism. I do not wish to interpret my skepticism negatively or to have it be so interpreted.

I have come to value my consciousness before all else and am well aware that its present disorder does not lend itself to rearrangement. A useless, harmful complexity; unproductive subtlety; paradox, deception, intoxication, disillusionment—all these I know as well as I know objects before my eyes. Yet I have never felt shame. True, I have felt an inexplicable anxiety at those moments when it seemed all too natural to be living with a consciousness so full of confusion and contradiction. I may even have expressed what sounded like an admission of shame. But I never really felt that emotion and believe that any possible expression of my shame came from a consciousness that was insufficiently disordered. An orderly consciousness will grasp an orderly truth; a moderate consciousness, a moderate truth. In the world of literature, truths of this kind are but fairy tales.

Never before in the literary history of our country has criticism seemed to occupy such a prominent position. Again, never before has such critical chaos reigned. But whereas from a bird's-eye view the situation looks chaotic, up close, focusing on the details, it appears orderly, if in a closefisted and grudging way. Some critics bemoan the loss of critical principles. But I would ask them, just once, to truly leave such principles behind.

At this moment when criticism is in chaos, who among our critics signals an awareness of how difficult it is to write criticism? The critical world is in turmoil, yet writing criticism seems to be as simple a task as it ever was. I want to focus on this bizarre situation. The crisis has nothing at all to do with any so-called loss of critical principles. Rather, what we see before us is a struggle among contending critics armed with a whole array of borrowed critical principles. Viewed from outside, the struggle looks chaotic. But does a sense of chaos exist within the spirit of each combatant? Does any real disorder exist there?

Since the appearance in the world of Aristotle's *Poetics*, the main thrust of his criticism was passed on from the Middle Ages through the Renaissance into modern times, without undergoing substantive change. The path taken by a host of critics had thus been an even one. Along this path, critics sang of the beauty of literary works classified by genre, or told the story of distinct aesthetic doctrines and principles. But with the emergence of the modern literary movement called Romanticism, it can be said that this level path ran into a mountain heretofore unknown.

The Romantics implanted the idea of relativism into literary criticism. No longer could critics see the crisp and clear outlines of a given literary work. Just behind the work loomed a human presence, as well as the place where that presence lived, and the history of its times. What had been an isolated and motionless literary work began to move before the critic's eye. The confusion thus visited on the practice of criticism lies at the origin of what we take to be literary criticism today. In other words, the determinedly modern, tragic shape assumed by Western literary criticism is a fact of past history and is already over a century old. It is no wonder, then, that critics, whose pronouncements were caught in the paradox-filled crosscurrents of the Romantic movement, who were passionate both to extol the creative freedom of the individual and to scientifically dispel all superstition, should have come to regard criticism itself with profound skepticism. It was startling for me to discover how closely related are the soliloquies of Sainte-Beuve and Gide.

The complications that modern literary criticism faced from the moment of its birth—the rivalry between creative and scientific impulses within the critical spirit—have not been resolved satisfactorily even in our own day. Perhaps we should say that these contradictory impulses have driven literature to become more and more specialized by type, so that each impulse is nurtured by a distinctive kind of writing spirit, and each one carries out its own solutions to literary problems. Only observe the difference in critical spirit between Plekhanov and Friche on the one hand, or Gundolf and Gide on the other.

Have these general complications within the modern critical spirit cast any sort of shadow over literary criticism in our country? We cannot find them, for example, in the criticism of Mori Ōgai, the greatest of our importers of Western writing. Even as our earliest critical battles were being waged by Ōgai and [Tsubouchi] Shōyō on the pages of *Shigarami zōshi* and *Waseda bungaku*, over such issues as idealism or its negation, or deductive against inductive methods, in Europe Taine and Pater were about to close their eyes in death. Later, we would witness [Takayama] Chogyū's intoxication with Nietzsche, [Shimamura] Hōgetsu's application of Arnold, [Ueda] Bin's emulation of Pater. Yet amid all this critical activity, no one questioned what made a literary work "literary." Symons was known, as were Gourmont and Anatole France, but the basic optimism of our critics showed no evidence of slipping from its base. The fact that Romanticism wreaked havoc with the spirit of classical criticism had no deep bearing on the history of modern literary criticism in our country. It is no exaggeration to say that down to the present, even in the area of criticism, not to speak of literature in general, the hand of science has not been felt at all.

Such were the conditions of literary criticism in Japan when suddenly a radically scientific method was introduced. I refer of course to Marxism. Although the historical fact of its introduction is not surprising in the least, it struck the literary world as a stunning event. Everyone was caught off guard, and so the reaction was indeed exaggerated. Amid all the distortions and bombast that marked this reaction, both those who imported the Marxist approach and those who just received it forgot the fact that no method even remotely similar to this one had ever been part of the critical traditions of Japan. This was a situation peculiar to our country, yet not a single critic pointed it out. Until this peculiarity is explained, it will remain impossible to fathom that complex farce currently enacted on many stages, whereby a critic is accused of being a "bourgeois liberal," never once having regarded himself consciously as such, yet on being so accused proudly claims that truly his criticism must be that of a bourgeois liberal.

But the farce thus born in the chaos of our critical condition will surely meet a farcical end unless our critics raise their level of awareness to see that the chaos itself is a product of conflicting critical paths. If our critics persist in seeing disorder as but the momentary reflection of a fleeting crisis, the disorder may well pass, having given birth to nothing.

I want to penetrate to the core of this disorder. I want to seize chaos as an opportunity and not hesitate to reach down to the roots of a question that is being posed for the first time in our literary history: Why is criticism a difficult thing? I do not intend to let go of this question, no matter what the outcome may be.

I do not want words like "chaos" and "disorder" to be the only ones used to describe the state of Japanese criticism today. Nor do I want such words to merely outline a critical scene wherein there is more than one kind of critic and a broad range of issues to address. I do mean to regard such descriptive language as a real enemy and threat to my spirit, as something I must overthrow. Still, it is not my belief that living with confusion is preferable to observing it. I simply want to feel whatever chaos is within myself as a living thing. By whatever means possible, I want to grapple with it hand to hand.

It may turn out that the chaos of our critical world will become all the more intense. Even for critics who believe that the enemy to be fought exists outside themselves, the time may come when they must face a host of enemies within. Like it or not, we will then need to experience at a deep level the real chaos, the actual disorder of our critical spirit.

2. On 'Watakushi shōsetsu'

In his literary review column in the December issue of *Bungei*, Kawakami Tetsutarō addressed himself to the issue of the *watakushi shōsetsu*. He cited a passage I had written in the inaugural issue of *Bungakkai*: "Balzac's novels are indeed fabricated, and precisely because they are fabricated, they are more splendid and more truthful than any confessional language about the artist's sufferings. Precisely because he overcame his self, and cast it aside, he discovered a path that was vital and alive within this fabrication." Kawakami went on to comment: "What is unfortunate is that Kobayashi concludes his essay with these words, when instead he should have begun his study of the *watakushi shōsetsu* with them." Kawakami is quite right. Still, my quoted words are extremely ambiguous. He might as well have criticized me, saying "Kobayashi should have begun his study of *orthodox realism* with them." At this point the issue suddenly expands, leaving us all in a stupefied haze. I lack the power, of course, to restore clarity, but reading Chikamatsu Shū-kō's "Kukai" (Sea of troubles) in the December issue of *Chūō kō-ron*, I feel compelled to return to the issue of personal fiction and try to draw out a bit more from my earlier remarks.

Writing in the *Tōkyō Asahi*, Uno Kōji praised "Kukai" as the most moving piece he had read in the past month. I, too, thought it extraordinary. But my feelings upon reading the story were so tangled and complex that even I could make no sense of them. First of all, I recognize straightaway that certain objections to the work—its style is old, its setting is narrow—are unsupportable, and that these very qualities make it plunge straight into the world of our emotions. At the same time, in the process of reading, I was aware of feeling somehow revolted and depressed. I will leave it to others to detail the extraordinary literary qualities of this story. However arrogant it may seem, I will try to focus on my feelings of depression.

Reading "Kukai," we understand the character of the man, Chikamatsu Shūkō. The man Chikamatsu seems neither greater nor lesser than the figure Tawara in the story. In that sense, perhaps "Kukai" is a story that has no secrets. I have met Chikamatsu only once, at a literary gathering, but reading this work I was made to recall Chikamatsu's expressions and movements at that time, especially the way he used his hand to massage a cramp in his leg. And I was given naturally to imagine, however disrespectful it may sound, the author making the rounds of the magazine offices in an effort to sell his work. How will I further describe my anxious feelings about this story, and where they have taken me?

Some will say that just such an anxious response to the work is proof of its quality. Perhaps. But such a positive claim, given the difficulties experienced by the reader, seems empty and remote. Will it further be claimed that what defines literature is just such remoteness? If that were so, then I would have no faith in literature. There is nothing in "Kukai" to make the heart feel refreshed, nothing to enrich one's sense of human life. Needless to say, it is

not the author's pessimistic spirit that leaves me dissatisfied. Even
pessimism, so long as it is powerfully expressed, has the capacity to
change lives. What I want to say is that in my reading experience,
"Kukai" possesses neither the power nor the true beauty of such
expression. The question is not whether a reading of "Kukai"
should bring the reader salvation. Rather, I want to ask Chikamatsu himself if he felt a writer's joy as he wrote it? Perhaps the
author would ask a question in turn—Who knows if literature is a
way toward enlightenment or delusion? But after nearly forty years
of life as a writer, it is unfortunate that joy, or if not joy, then a fierce
pride becoming to a writer, should have left no mark on him. Of
course we cannot say that there are many writers, who, having
risked a lifetime of discontent, are unmistakably stamped with
such a mark. But precisely because we know that they exist, we
maintain hope in literature, knowing full well how much discontent it will continue to generate.

"Kukai" runs counter to such a hope. But would we be better off
and feel less guilty, had we read a work possessing sweeter sentiments?

The progenitor of the I-novel was no doubt Jean-Jacques Rousseau. At least he was the first to be clearly conscious of the question of the confessional self, and to make it part of literature. The
unhappiness he outlined in his *Confessions* is not that of a hero,
but of a common man. Yet readers often find this unhappiness beyond their grasp. To put it another way, they sense in the writing a
power that redeemed the author's unhappy existence. This power
reveals an "I," and salvages something greater than "I." The author
writes an autobiography, and turns it into literature. In other
words, the objectivity of the *Confessions* rests on the author's belief in his unprecedented project: to speak without reserve about
himself. And what inspired such belief was a prior conviction that
if society was a problem for him, then a man like himself was
surely a problem for society.

His strategy was a clear and simple one. To overcome himself, he
would speak about himself as honestly as possible. Perhaps the
magnificent drama enacted in the *Confessions* seems a bit too un-
adorned and simple to us, obsessed as we have become with theories about the *watakushi shōsetsu*. But we should also realize that

all kinds of questions about the I-novel are strewn along a great road that begins and ends with Rousseau.

Kawakami Tetsutarō has described two conditions that spawned the I-novel. Of the first, he writes: "Among the various anxieties felt by the writer as he seeks ways to effectively depict a certain fictional persona, the clear majority owe less to the writer trying to break away from the persona than to his attempt to break away from himself. We can thus affirm a common phenomenon, whereby as art advances, the wish to break away from the self manifests a powerful latent energy." And of the second: "At the same time it can be said that the artist is obsessed with an inwardly glimpsed image of himself." Kawakami concludes, stating that "until now, our conception of the I-novel has been based on only the latter of these two conditions." I think this is a fair assessment, although these two conditions are so entangled that we cannot easily say which one is more dominant, because both are essential to the writer's spirit, trying to express itself by means of a certain fascination with the self. Here we grasp a double-edged sword. Thus, even within Kawakami's second condition, a double-sided outline appears.

However, reading a *watakushi shōsetsu*, I immediately gauge what might be called the distance between the real life of the author and the author of the work. The question is not one of depth, that is, the degree of sincerity an author conveys, but rather one of breadth—how wide is the gap, the distance between the two? If one focuses instead on depth of feeling, then immediately the question is rendered personal, and made more complicated. Take, for example, Hirotsu Kazuo's recent critique of the [Tokuda] Shūsei story, "Shi ni shitashimu" (Intimate with death) in the November issue of *Bungei shunjū*, which follows this trajectory as far as Hirotsu's curiosity takes him. But were we to see the question instead as one of writing, trying to gauge the gap between real life and the author, then we could clarify any number of abstract issues as they relate to the *watakushi shōsetsu*. The fact that I once praised Uno Kōji's "Ko no raireki" (Annals of a child) has less to do with the shadow cast on the story by the scenery of real life than with the distance between what the author of that work clearly felt and the personal life of Uno. It is a distance that is bracing, exhilarating. But in the case of "Shi ni shitashimu," there is less distance, and lesser still in "Kukai." As for the issue of the real feelings and sentiments of Shūkō, Shūsei, or Uno—I have no idea whose run deepest.

In the headnote to his literary review in the *Tōkyō Asahi*, Uno cited the following passage from Shiga Naoya: "As I gaze upon the Merciful Kannon at the Yumedono, it does not occur to me to ask who created this statue. This is because the statue possesses a life wholly apart from its creator. It is unique. If from literature I were able to create such a work, I would never think to attach my name to it." In these words of our preeminent author of *watakushi shō-setsu*, who combines a primitive desire for life with a classical sensibility, there is not the slightest metaphorical significance. Like Uno, I number these words among the most beautiful Shiga ever wrote, yet am not inclined to rummage through them for some significance that might resolve the "I-novel" controversy which presently besets us. In fact, Shiga's aesthetics are not strong enough to settle this question. It is also true that his aesthetics shape his moral understanding.

"I thought the work was interesting. But then I met the author, and found out he was a bore . . ." Statements like this abound, although I will not trade here in such critical vulgarities. Still, I question if in Japan today there are many writers whose fictional worlds have excavated a depth that is not wholly apparent in real life. Isn't it the case that for most of our writers, literature has not disentangled itself from real life? And isn't real life greater than fiction for most writers? Not only did such questions go unasked in the tradition of I-novel writing; they were avoided out of desperation. Our writers chewed real life to the bone, exhausting its possibilities, yet remain bewitched by their dream of "real life," and have now seized upon a territory called "deep feelings." But what are readers given to chew in these stories? To be blunt, we are being fed leftovers. Meanwhile, those who continued writing in bondage to real life knew that even as the plenitude of this real life was being depleted, so too were their dreams of literature. It was at this juncture that the Merciful Kannon of the Yumedono appeared.

I am neither contemptuous of the sphere of sensibility that our established writers attained, nor feel the least envy of their position. Nor do I have any faith in Marxist literature, although I do value the ambition to create social novels, something Marxism evoked. I believe in the passion to write for others, having abandoned the self. Again, although I have no faith in psychological novels or in novels of ideas, I do believe that such novelists, whose dreams of creating a viable self-portrait were dashed as abruptly as were their dreams of suckling on real life, are still stirred by an ambition to break new literary ground. At present, the *watakushi shōsetsu* is being destroyed from two directions. The writer is either overcome by ideology and abandons his self without a fight before discovering any new face to portray in his work, or else he destroys his portrait under pressure from his surroundings and can find no inner imperative to build a new literature. The chaos thus loosed on our fiction is analogous to the chaos of our critical world and is becoming more and more intense. Seedlings and sprouts are everywhere. But nothing stands.

What should be the reply if asked what was the year's unequivocal masterpiece? I myself would agree with those who say it is Tanizaki's "Shunkinshō" (Portrait of Shunkin). I would also admit to the strangeness of our times, the absurdity of our cultural situation, as well as to our unending hope.

I am moved to re-read all of Dostoevsky. This author did not utter a word about his real life, suffused though it was with a depth and range of vital experience. When he had exhausted the bounty of real life, he created a rich literature. All of his writing is replete with secrets drawn from real life, yet we cannot read his fiction without dismissing as abject lies the records of real life kept by his wife and daughter. In just such a writer I believe we find the richest, most fertile field wherein to explore issues of the I-novel. In every possible way, I want to engage the secrets of this writer.

Discourse on Fiction of the Self

(May–August 1935)

I have resolved on an enterprise which has no imitator. My purpose is to display to my kind a portrait in every way true to nature, and the man I shall portray will be myself.

Simply myself. I know my own heart and understand my fellow man. But I am made unlike anyone I have ever met; I will even venture to say that I am like no one in the whole world. I may be no better, but at least I am different. Whether Nature did well or ill in breaking the mould in which she formed me, is a question which can only be resolved after the reading of my book.

This is, of course, the famous opening of Rousseau's *Confessions*. For the moment I will not question the grandiloquence of this language. And I regard it of no great consequence whether, in this unprecedented work, Rousseau succeeded in speaking authentically about himself. In such later writing as "Dreams of a Solitary Wanderer," we can well appreciate the state toward which this self, previously sacrificed on the altar of Nature, had been driven. Rather, what I want to call attention to is that in the context of modern fiction, the "I-novel" finds its originating source in the excesses of Rousseau's language. Without this cry at the beginning of his *Confessions*, such distinguished I-novels as *Werther*, *Obermann*, and *Adolphe*, would never have been born.

We can begin by saying that an "I-novel" is a sincere self-confession written in fictional prose. At first glance it would also seem that in the novel's formative years, all writers had recourse to this method of writing. But history is strange, and until a sense of the individual had grown to become of profound human significance, a fiction of the self did not appear in European literary history. Recalling, too, that Rousseau was a European of the eighteenth century, we might well ask when, and with what sort of birth cry, did our own I-novel come into being? The question arises because the I-novel, which emerged at the vanguard of the Romantic movement in the West, did not exist in Japanese literature. People began to speak of *watakushi shōsetsu* only after our Naturalist movement had reached maturity.

I

In the end I am not persuaded that art creates other fictional lives. I possess none of the grand, transcendental views about art that were shared by the literary youth of a previous generation. I see art simply as the re-presentation of the experiences of a single human life. . . .

For example, in the case of Balzac, no matter how hard he struggled to depict an expansive "human comedy," to create life-like human characters such as the usurer or the grande dame, his work yet strikes me as mere fabrication. I cannot trust this fabrication, although I can trust the little Balzac has to say about the artist's sufferings. A great writer depicts others and allows his self to wander without restraint, even though only a few such geniuses have ever lived. However, I believe the moment one assumes the guise of another, a certain distance, a certain expedient duplicity, whether we ascribe it to technique or embellishment, attends the artwork. No matter then how wonderful it is to read, I cannot finally trust it. And so at a recent public lecture, I made the controversial remark that Tolstoy's *War and Peace*, Dostoevsky's *Crime and Punishment*, and Flaubert's *Madame Bovary*, however high their quality, are mere popular novels. They are, after all, fabrications, literary entertainment.

This citation is from a review Kume Masao wrote in 1923. I quote Kume's opinions not because I think they are insightful, but because according to our vantage they may reveal something of genuine interest. It would be perfectly correct to say that these are just Kume's personal opinions, or that they are opinions shared by a large number of our contemporary writers. But it is even truer to say that Kume's words directly point to an almost unconscious conviction hidden deep within our minds. For when he wrote this, discussions about the I-novel had in fact become discussions about pure literature.

The plausibility of his views notwithstanding, by its outspokenness Kume's criticism moves us toward an unavoidable fact; namely, that because our Naturalist fiction was so dominant, truly distinguished Western writing came to be regarded as vulgar entertainment. Perhaps it was beyond the ability of the parties to the I-novel debates to seriously engage the question of the peculiar fate of the I-novel in this country. But how is it that our critics today, confident that they already opened up a broad field of literary vision, should have overlooked so much? For the fact remains that our critics have overlooked a great deal, and are presently making the absurd claim that discussions about a fiction of the self are passé. Such fissures in critical understanding, peculiar to our situation, have appeared throughout modern Japanese literary history. It is time to distance ourselves from discussions of critical methods (how appallingly derivative of Western critical methods are our own!) and, fixing these gaps and fissures clearly in our sight, take action.

In France, too, it happened that as the Naturalist movement reached its own dominant phase, there arose a literary movement calling for a fiction of the self. We see this in Barres and, later, in Gide and Proust. Regardless of the pinnacle of achievement each of these writers attained, they were all motivated by the desire to regenerate a human nature rendered stiff and conventional by the pressures of nineteenth-century Naturalist thought. And they were not mistaken to undertake a literary investigation of the self to achieve this, because already by that time, their literary "I" was a fully socialized one.

In his *Confessions*, Rousseau never imagined he was simply portraying his own real life, much less did he torment himself trying to give it clever expression. He was stirred by the question of what significance the individual has in society and, ultimately, by a passionate feeling for the place of man in nature. It may or may not be appropriate to call the *Confessions* an "I-novel" (Mr. Kume has already addressed this issue). The important fact is that Rousseau's ideas inform Goethe, Sénancour, and Constant, even where there exists no obvious influence, and even if these writers do not directly imitate Rousseau's style. No matter how deeply the protagonists of these I-novels probe the meaning of their personal lives, in their authors' minds an explicit conflict existed between the individual and nature, or again, between the individual and society. As a consequence, the Naturalist writers who later emerged had all passed through an intellectual training predicated on this conflict. Adhering to the logic of positivism, what became the Naturalist enterprise of penetrating the self through a portrayal of others was not so rare and unusual an activity as to have attracted, as Kume would have it, only the genius.

In the end, the Naturalist movement in Japan fostered a distinctive form of writing about the self, and not for some inherent reason, such as the so-called temperament of the Japanese people. It was owing primarily to this fact; namely, that the external, social conditions present when the I-novel emerged in the West were not present here. Naturalist writing was imported, but not only was our version of a modern bourgeois society too small-scale to nurture the ideology of positivism that supported European Naturalism, there were in addition too many old and outmoded kinds of fertilizer in the cultural ground here.

Of course even if the ground is not prepared for the cultivation of new ideas, people can still use them to become intoxicated. This occurred in Russia around the middle of the nineteenth century, when nearly every young writer went about gesturing madly. Our writers did not always exhibit such signs. It is not that they could not get drunk, just that they felt no need to do so. They may not have been living in a society suited to the maintenance of Western ideas, but they did possess an old and powerful literary tradition that had no parallel in Russia or certain other non-European countries. Consciously or not, our writers lived in the presence of splendid literary techniques, so that there was no force in groundless Western ideas to move them. And because they possessed a consummate sense of literary aesthetics, there was nothing more natural or pleasurable for our writers than to dissolve a newly imported idea in a mixture of native literary techniques. Our

Naturalists were safely positioned to perform this natural and pleasurable experiment. Please understand that I mean "safely positioned" with regard to literary practice and ideas, not with respect to their actual lives.

Inspired by a reading of Maupassant's short stories, Tayama Katai once wrote: "Until now I had fixed my gaze on Heaven, yearning for higher things. I knew nothing about the earth, absolutely nothing. What a shallow idealist I was! But from this moment I wish to be a child of the earth, proud to crawl along the ground like an animal, never again so vain as to wish for the stars."

What was it in Maupassant that inspired Katai? It was neither the wretchedness of Maupassant's life, nor his despair and loneliness as a writer. If anything intoxicated Katai, it was Maupassant's fresh writing style, which turned away from Heaven to inspect the earth.

Yet behind Maupassant's work was a spirit that had been annihilated by the unfeeling ideology of the age, the covetous dreams of the French bourgeoisie, that required every manner of thing to be measured and rendered useful by science, and that already had led Flaubert to despair of human nature, driving him to a conscious detachment from the real world. The "I" that would appear in their literary work was thus an "I" already dead. Because they could believe no longer in either a personal or a social life, of necessity they invented a new fictional style. Even Flaubert's renowned "Madame Bovary, c'est moi" is the expression of someone who perforce recognized that although his "self" was alive in the literary work, in reality it was no more.

Zola appears to have taken a quite different path. Instead of reviling the ideology of the age, he freely embraced it, yet in doing so arrived at the same point of losing the "I" of his personal life. There were no doubt countless people in the late nineteenth century who cleverly manipulated ideas to satisfy practical needs. However, the construction of an artistic monument to ideas requires the ruination of lives, like Zola's, that were ideology-obsessed. And so the relationship between Zola and Claude is not dissimilar to the relationship between Flaubert and Madame Bovary.

These battles over ideas waged by French writers were the most difficult things for our importers of Naturalism to comprehend:

"When I began my creative life, I needed some source of inspiration, because my ideas, approach, and style were virtually unconnected to Japanese literary history. Tokugawa writing did not excite me. [Ozaki] Kōyō and [Kōda] Rohan were no influence. If I now ask myself where I looked for a source of inspiration, I would answer—Wordsworth."

These are the words of [Kunikida] Doppo, but every Japanese writer since the middle of the Meiji period worked in the grip of his own Wordsworth. Each had his own beloved Wordsworth, or Zola, or Maupassant, or Flaubert. How do we explain this? Plainly our writers took in a range of ideas that were contained within the styles of these Western writers. Still, such ideas only cultivated each writer's fantasy. Foreign ideas did not exist beyond style, because our writers were only looking at them in terms of style. What we absorbed were not ideas but impressions. And this was quite expedient.

Maupassant's work, itself distanced from the author's real life, gave to Katai the compass by which to orient his own life, and gave him happiness. The secret behind the later emergence of a whole genre of criticism designed to discuss a fiction of the self—*watakushi shōsetsu ron*—is to be located within the strange circumstances of the composition of Katai's *Futon* (The quilt), which initiated the I-novel in our country. At least theoretically, the outlines of this secret are very clear: no matter how gifted, a Japanese writer could not single-handedly create the spirit of the age or its social ideology. Similarly, no matter how insipid or trivial the imported ideology, the writer could not rediscover or reinvent it here. It was left to the writer to clarify or to actualize in his work the ideas already existing among the people. At this level, some ideas seemed as hard as material objects, others as pliant as human beings. Still, only if ideas are understood to be part of a living reality, can they become the writer's proper enemy or proper friend. When Katai discovered Maupassant, he was unable to comprehend the power of an idea that existed outside literature yet was strongly at work either to inhibit or to incite his literary activity. Emerging outside yet impinging itself on literature, the power of an idea, once it was institutionalized and socialized, began to function almost organically—a phenomenon beyond the capacity of Japanese writers to fathom even in their dreams. For the writer who forbid himself to "wish for the stars of Heaven," it was natural to turn in the direction of real life, expecting it to supply the basic material for literature, as well as a satisfactory foundation on which to build a new conception of human nature. After Katai, fiction closely adhered to the facts of the author's real life, even as it demonstrated startling technical advances, particularly in the nuanced depiction of fictional character. As for the self-sufficient [Shimazaki] Tōson's "revolutionary" *Hakai* or [Tokuda] Shūsei's "decadent" *Arakure*, it may be correct to describe the technical, stylistic aspects of their work as being "revolutionary" or "decadent," whether or not these authors intended such effects or seriously confronted social issues.

Here we trace the path that connects the earlier *watakushi shōsetsu* to the more recent *shinkyō shōsetsu*. A tale based on a personal experience or a personal confession, as it becomes increasingly refined, tends toward a purified "I." And the significance of the use by the literati in the 1920's of terms such as "fiction of the self" and "pure fiction" interchangeably, is to be located here as well.

Ōgai and Sōseki were not part of the *watakushi shōsetsu* movement, nor did they share its fate. They were writers of extraordinary cultivation and taste, who no doubt perceived the abnormalities within our Naturalist, confessionalist fiction. Akutagawa was the principal inheritor of their perceptions in this regard. It is a matter of great sadness that Akutagawa was constitutionally unable to endure this legacy. Yet has the Akutagawa tragedy ended with his death? In what form does a fiction of the self appear before our eyes today?

2

"As I gaze upon the Merciful Kannon at the Yumedono, it does not occur to me to ask who created this statue. This is because the statue possesses a life wholly apart from its creator. It is unique. If from literature I were able to create such a work, I would never think to attach my name to it."

This passage is from the preface Shiga Naoya wrote for a collection of his short stories, published in 1928. Nothing I have ever read so beautifully and simply captures the essential meaning of *watakushi shōsetsu*. Whether Shiga will ever write something he "would never think to attach [his] name to" need not concern us here. More significant is the long silence that followed upon Shiga's arrival at this sentiment.

Not since Katai learned from Maupassant the literary value of mundane life, has anyone so intensely and splendidly rendered aesthetic his own life as has Shiga Naoya. No writer has with such scrupulous single-mindedness followed the path of *watakushi shōsetsu*, wherein theories about daily life would become, without mediation, theories of artistic creation. As Shiga stood in profound contemplation before the Merciful Kannon in the Yumedono, his work arrived at its proper destination. This purification of his daily life dispelled the many problems and crises that had formerly beset him. At this point he no longer had need of his actual life as a working companion. No matter how the author himself might explain it, behind the silence of this writer there must have been both the tranquillity of a man who had exhausted the resources of real life, and the pain of a novelist who had lost the most familiar material for his expression.

It was Flaubert's sense as well that he would not think to attach his name to his work: "The artist is someone who must conduct himself so as to make posterity believe that he never existed in this world." But at the age of twenty-four, he also wrote: "The only way to escape misfortune is to remain in seclusion with art. All else is unavailing. I have neither wealth nor love nor desire nor regret. I have totally divorced myself from real life." It would be well for us to note how strangely this compares to the case of Shiga, for whom the desire to save himself from the dangers of real life became, without qualification, the central motif of his creative work; moreover, the perfection of his work was not at all sacrificed in this process.

Of course Shiga is the archetypal example, and his extraordinary scrupulousness makes clear the crisis that awaits the writer who would walk the path of rendering aesthetic his personal life. For the writer there was a necessary proximity to this crisis, once the seeds sown at the birth of the *watakushi shōsetsu* had matured. What is so striking about Shiga is that he caused these seeds, sown by others earlier, to mature straightaway. Yet every baptized Naturalist had encountered a similar crisis, and was constrained by it. Someone like Shimazaki Tōson has overcome this dangerous proximity to actual life by a heart-and-soul devotion to historical projects. Others, like Masamune Hakuchō, have warily eyed the danger and kept it at bay with an impressionistic essay style. And there are those too like Tokuda Shūsei who have achieved a degree of creative autonomy paradoxically, by allowing the story to be told by an uncommon life-force, by entrusting the story to the unrefined habits of unmediated life experience.

It is well known that the Taishō period was marked by the resistance of many writers, mounted from a variety of positions, to the *watakushi shōsetsu* as it had developed since the Meiji period. *Shirakaba-ha, Shinkankaku-ha, Waseda-ha, Mita-ha*—there were all manner of adversarial voices, yet nowhere was heard a voice rejecting unequivocally a fiction of the self. Perhaps no one had read with genuine terror Flaubert's reflections on the novel, which had provoked him to declare, at the age of twenty-four, that he would henceforth take leave of real life. To the contrary, the Taishō voices of opposition commonly shared a certain trust in everyday experience as the wellspring of their creative activity (a trust Meiji authors themselves had possessed), along with a sense that everyday experience was the richest source of the dreams that would inform their writing. And so this Taishō "resistance" to the I-novel was really passive, each writer's new psychological or sensual or intellectual gloss upon or manipulation of real life expressing itself as opposition. This common perspective made it hard to distinguish one writer's work from another. Still, it is clear that this passive opposition compelled writers, under various guises, to ascend the same predestined road as had been climbed by a previous generation of I-novelists. And on this road they all encountered the same danger: that theories about everyday experience, and theories about artistic creation, would collide.

Perhaps it is not strange that over time both Kikuchi Kan and Kume Masao, who had emerged as the brightest and ablest among those who opposed the existing Naturalist novel, would come to regard popular literature as the proper locus of their work. This shift represents neither a slackening nor a breakdown of the writer's conscience, as certain sentimentalists would have it. A nicely balanced paradox predicated their abandonment of pure literature. On the one hand, they could not help but believe that everyday experience remained the stuff of pure literature; on the other, they had no real faith in the process of rendering aesthetic such experience. The Naturalist *watakushi shōsetsu*, which was also referred to as an "objective novel," had hidden within it a certain Romanticism, a longing that art would become, in Kume's phrase, "the savior of life." Both Kume and Kikuchi, whose work began as intellectualized commentary on everyday experience, possessed a fresh vision that ran counter to this type of *watakushi shōsetsu*. The robust common sense of Kikuchi detected the narrowness of the world that remained to write about, once one had embarked on a way of literature committed to the aestheticization of the author's life. And it was the vivid, lush sensibility of Kume that registered revulsion before the tragedy and torment of this literary way. That both writers finally were willing to sacrifice the purity of literature in an attempt to socialize it by resort to popular writing marks less an intentional than a natural process.

In an article he wrote recently, titled "Pure Literature as Dilettantism" (April, *Bungei shunjū*), Kume begins by saying that "it is not my aim to engage in any sort of fashionable, paradox-filled phrase-making, because I believe there is some truth to what I am about to say," and goes on to state that pure literature is dilettantish, the plaything of amateurs. He claims that it is fundamentally mistaken to try to make pure literature a profession. Putting aside a real question—Is there any quality in such "professional" writing?—it is still reasonable to suggest that a pure literature, not subject to coercion from external forces, does at least possess autonomy. Moreover, as Kume states, if pure literature is a dilettante's game of emotional revelation, it makes no sense to contend that it requires a real-life sacrifice. Again, putting aside the real question as to whether writers so foolishly misguided ever produced quality writing, it is reasonable to admit, as the saying goes, that "good manners take a full stomach." What is telling about our present situation is that young writers are driven into literary activity without the wherewithal to make such reasonable observations. Time flows in strange ways. There is considerable distance, for example, between Kume's conception of "living," and what our younger writers take it to mean, and this should be examined. Regardless of the rigor or the logic of Kume's essay, it represents a reiteration of his long-held wish to render aesthetic his personal life and to discover a purified form of personal fiction. It contains the reminiscences of a man who, well after his consciousness of being an amateur had bested his sense of being a pure writer, continues to describe, in the accents of a dilettante, a state he repeatedly experienced, that of "waking from a dream in the dark of night, chilled to the bone."

Tanizaki Jun'ichirō and Satō Haruo were among the most agile at resisting the Naturalist *watakushi shōsetsu*. Both writers are often labeled "Romantic," but all this means is that Tanizaki portrays life as an epic of the senses, and Satō portrays it as a psychological lyric. It is widely noticed these days that Tanizaki has undergone a significant transformation, reflected both in his attitude toward literary creation and in his style, beginning with *Mōmoku monogatari* (A blind man's tale). In a recent review in *Chūō kōron*, Ikuta Chōkō indicts the weakness and insufficiency of this "classical style" as recently promoted by Tanizaki. Ikuta argues that such a style is too constrained and fragile to support modern fiction. The charge itself has merit, although Ikuta's rhetoric is truly leaden and predictable. At first glance, such reviews seem to be confronting an issue head on, but in fact they just press their unwanted attentions upon a given writer. Tanizaki knows perfectly well what his literary position is and what his stylistic decisions represent.

More important, his "great reformation" would have been quite hopeless were he unaware of how this style that he was at pains to cultivate could function as a stylistic theory for modern fiction. What should concern us is not the degree of perfection of this style. Rather, the crucial issue turns on Tanizaki's having lost interest, or claiming to have lost interest, in what we call modern fiction. Were Tanizaki to reform his style yet again in accordance with Ikuta's suggestions, his readers would be distressed. Fortunately, this is not about to happen. Tanizaki's reformation is not an intellectual matter susceptible to the advice of critics. His is an unavoidably decadent art that triumphs over the crisis faced by a man who has exhausted his taste for real life. Moreover, Tanizaki was driven toward this style by society. We should rather question if it were possible for Tanizaki to further refine mundane life, beyond the refinements he had achieved in *Tade kuu mushi* (Some prefer nettles), and not trouble ourselves over the question of what sort of style properly represents modern writing.

In the case of Satō, we recognize that his conception of fiction is at a stalemate, once the author's personal life has been exhaustively lyricized. Several of his long works sought to negotiate this crisis, but without success. Presently Satō seems beset by the following question: Should he erect a barrier against the surrounding world of confusion and disorder and look to history for his dreams? Even were I wrong about this question facing Satō, at the very least it can be said that his internal logic, which had purged the sensibility that informed his early work, extinguished as well its vigor.

And so it happened that the first solid resistance to the fictionalization of the writer's mundane life came with the introduction of Marxist writing. What was being imported was no longer a literary style, but a social ideology. It is quite clear that modern Japanese fiction encountered something genuinely new when it imported this ideology, as a structure indissolubly absolute and universal, that affected both the literary world at large and the styles of individual writers. If the genuine novelty of this event is not grasped, it becomes all the more difficult to make sense of the ensuing discord that it provoked in the *bundan*.

When an ideology is imbued with a universal aspect, resisting every local interpretation put forward by individual writers, we encounter socialized thought in its primary form. Our young writers could not help becoming intoxicated on this strange new substance. It is obvious that Marxist criticism surpassed proletarian fictional achievement, and came to occupy a position of creative leadership. Never before had writers labored to create by relying so on ideas and theories; again, never before had writers so completely ignored their actual, physical lives. It is not just that they had forgotten how to embody or to internalize an idea. Rather, being intoxicated on a system of thought too bloodless to allow any real internalization or embodiment, our Marxist literary movement was defined, in essence, by its intoxicating effects.

And so these writers came to ignore not only earlier writing and past literary relations, but also certain inherited tendencies within themselves. It all led to the same thing—the writer's difficulty in reading his situation—yet there was no consciousness of this difficulty. Indeed, if writers had become conscious in this way, their literary activity would have come to a halt. Shall we question whether these ideologues were right or wrong in their theories? It seems to me they simply did what they had to do.

As suitable material for fiction, our newly rising Marxist writers rejected mundane life, the very mundane life that the Naturalists, together with their so-called adversaries, had expended such efforts on, to observe, interpret, and represent. It wasn't that the young Marxists had lost the old feel for daily life, but that their ideology instructed them to transform the concept of "life" from the mundane into the historical. They began to look at everything through this transformed perspective. Now, to look at something means to adopt or to reject, to choose one thing and not another. Observation, in other words, signifies a certain liquidation of possibility. The young Marxists were not oblivious to self-reflection. It was just that their "selves" were not suitable for reflection. What they revealed when they did attempt to reflect on their selves, was a petit-bourgeois consciousness about everything. And so the catchword "liquidation" really signified a concealment. It covered over the various deceptions and adventures involved when emotion, sensation, and ideas try to discover self-reflection anew.

Because they believed that their ideology was corroborated by a subtle positivism, Marxist writers remained unaware (perhaps they wished to remain unaware) of their intellectual anxiety. And they never questioned the politicization of their literary theories because their ideology advanced the claim of such theories to political leadership on criteria again based on empirical experience. Thus there emerged the well-known, widely heralded notion that a difference exists between "proletarian" and "Marxist" writing.

Still, the fictional mode everyone believed in was realism. Marxist critics stressed the point that this realism was not bourgeois realism, indeed that it was intrinsically different, although they were hard put to spell out these differences, much less explain the distinction between a "humanistic" and a "social scientific" fictional character. Work began to flood the market that took no account of the stylistic methods devised by certain Taishō writers opposed to the Naturalist realism of their own day. Even the psychological approach, available since the emergence of modern realism, was seldom used. As farms and factories came to loom large as the content of fiction, the attention to form grew thin. In fact, some came to think that any formalism that affected writing practice was to be rejected.

There is an issue here that should not be obscured. However paradoxical it sounds, I believe such writers subsisted on sheer formalism, even though they denounced it themselves. Theory is, in the first instance, a matter of form. When an idea does not possess a universally communicable form, it has no capacity to influence society. Marxist writers had vitality precisely because they believed in these formal characteristics of thought. Indeed, their achievements should be valued, and not reduced to the tedious question of what brand of formalism they represented, because they single-handedly undertook a project without precedent in our literary world; namely, to import a system of thought with its essential elements intact.

Perhaps the Marxists will not leave a single literary masterpiece to posterity. Perhaps much that goes on in their fiction is just a gathering of fantasy "people." But this should not be characterized as fictional success or failure owing to a given writer's peculiar taste or style. It has rather to do with fiction becoming twisted by ideology, with literary proportions becoming bloated on theory.

Japanese Naturalism is less a bourgeois than a feudal style of writing, and, contrary to the finest works of Western Naturalism that reflect a sense of historical time, the most distinguished of our Naturalist *watakushi shōsetsu* reveal the limpid visage of a single persona. What the proletarian writers erased was this visage. Who can deny that a certain purifying erasure, through the force of ideology, occurs in all Marxist writing? Compared to their literary victory over a predetermined literary temperament, their alleged inability to vividly depict the attitudes and tastes of fictional characters seems a matter of far lesser significance.

3

Yokomitsu Riichi has caused a stir in the *bundan* with his recent "Junsui shōsetsu ron" (Essay on pure fiction). One can easily imagine why this style of psychological analysis would have provoked a series of niggling controversies, although it should be understood that at the moment, any clarifying, hard-edged debate is impossible in the first place. Still, we detect in Yokomitsu's essay an idea or a longing of a kind that has shaped this author's thoughts and feelings for some time. It is not an essay written on a whim. To express his ideas, Yokomitsu has coined a number of terms, although it may prove beyond anyone's capacity to find a clearing through these entanglements in his language.

Of course ideas about pure fiction begin with André Gide. The reason Gide has come to occupy such a pivotal place in the world of modern French letters is to be found in his spirit of passionate self-inquiry: "I wrote this at a time when I felt the literary air had grown frighteningly stale. It seemed to me a matter of profound urgency to make literature come into contact anew with the great earth, to let it walk barefoot through the fields."

This is from Gide's preface to *Fruits of the Earth*, written in 1897, in other words, several years before our literary world expressed its wonder and admiration for Maupassant. Indeed, after reading Maupassant, Katai felt it necessary to have literature "walk barefoot through the fields." Need we demonstrate the difference between the French sense of "barefoot" and Katai's use of the word? Rather, we should question whether Japanese writers could fathom Gide's condition of mind, his felt need to fulminate against the "stale" literary air, even as French Naturalist fiction reached full maturity, attaining the objectivity requisite for an expansive, social novel.

Nineteenth-century positivism disposed of the self, made it a victim of ideology, and, except for a very few writers who detected traces of the self in art, made the average writer stale. But just when the richness of interiority was being most sorely neglected, and the expression of personal desire was growing weak, Gide sought to obliterate all else and restore faith in the self. He determined to create within his own nature a laboratory where he would discover how much skepticism, how much complexity, how much luxury and confusion, self-consciousness could endure. Surrounding Gide was the inertia of an enervated literary environment, full of catchwords like "objective position" or "scientific observation," amid which a superficial belief in the non-subjective led to a superficial belief about literature. Alone, Gide set out on a different path. His splendid gesture taught people to turn their eyes toward that observation of the self that takes place before any writing.

Katai's decision to let literature walk barefoot on the earth is remote from any idealism regarding the observation of human nature. His distance from idealism permitted him to discover his new path in a literary technique, and this discovery in turn became the theory that gave substance to his personal life. For Gide the situation was notably different. When he referred to a "barefoot" literature, he meant neither to oppose earlier literary methods nor to propose a new literary attitude. Rather, he revealed an awareness that literature could not be trusted unconditionally, and that self-consciousness could not exist in servitude to literature. For Katai on the other hand, belief in the self connoted belief in a personal life and in personal fiction. These are quite different perceptions. Here we observe the distance separating the image of the self that attracted our authors of *watakushi shōsetsu*, and the self that enticed Gide and the French.

Our I-novelists felt not the least anxiety about their belief in the self and in personal life because the world of the self, without mediation, assumed for them the shape of society. And so the *watakushi shōsetsu* turned decadent on a subtle mixture of the dregs of the feudal self and feudal society. Gide was haunted by the self for quite different reasons. Because both Rousseau and Zola existed in his past, he could not be satisfied with a bombastic confession that attacked society or with a depiction of society that disregarded the individual. It was in this context that he built his laboratory of self-consciousness. What obsessed him was not the figure of the self but the problems it posed. The issue of individuality, the place of the individual, became the wellspring for his activity. This laboratory work led to yet another discovery, a certain mechanism that calibrated the intake of the individual and the social into literature.

Amid the social crisis provoked by the Great War, many young artists and writers despaired over creating art. But Gide's work matured steadily. Of course no writer was so consumed by anxiety or, from within anxiety, so tirelessly measured the bounds of literary possibility. He opened his laboratory to everything. And inside it, where multiple ideas and passions flowed in uncontrollably, Gide never doubted that he had found a site of creativity that would ever yield pleasurable sensations of terror or fright. What always surprises me as I read Gide is his obstinate affection for such instability. Yet it was precisely because of this affection that his anxiety did not degenerate into either a comedy of ideas or an intellectualized farce. It also permitted a certain vital optimism to be felt even in his literature of anxiety.

Gide is neither a dilettante nor a skeptic, just someone who has lived out a radical relativism. For him, writing that adheres to a clearly defined ideology or to specific material things would not be possible. As Edouard remarks in *The Counterfeiters*: "'A slice of life' the Naturalist school said. The great defect of that school is that it always cuts its slice in the same direction; in time, lengthwise. Why not in breadth? Or in depth? As for me, I should not like to cut at all." And Gide continues: "I invent the character of a novelist, whom I make my central figure; and the subject of the book, if you must have one, is precisely that struggle between what reality offers him and what he himself intends to make of it."

If we read *The Counterfeiters* as the working out of Gide's ideas on the pure novel, we see that the book offers us a totally new standard of measurement. Here is a style of realism so direct and reliable that it seems unaffected by the psychological or impressionistic methods popular in literary circles. What Edouard tells us about his own way of cutting a "slice of life," how he would use the scissors, is marvelously realized in the novel as a whole. Although Edouard said that he "should not like to cut at all," this is of course a practical impossibility. As we might expect, *The Counterfeiters* reveals both horizontal and vertical cuts—the figure of a cross. In the process of reading, we come upon a countless number of such cuts, just as in the course of our lives we endure any number of worldly gashes.

To be sure, there are dimensions to an actual event that could never appear in fiction, no matter how faithfully the writer sought to describe them. Something happens, and in an instant a multitude surrounds the event: those who immediately witness it, those who hear about it indirectly, those who are emotionally affected by it, and so forth. Nothing happens in isolation. And in the reverberating cries that well up all around it, the event reveals a countless number of "cuts." According to Edouard, the earlier realist novel was too thick-skinned to feel these innumerable cuts. It would seem that writers possessed of a universalist idea can only imagine a single way of cutting. Yet the very fact that an incalculable number of people exist who understand this universalist idea in an incalculable number of ways, gives the idea life in society. And so those who take pleasure, say, in a formalist idea, could not live a life drained of the proclivities and whimsical tastes suited to the cultivation of it.

Authors create fictional types who possess a certain character, a certain passion or spiritual motivation. But all of them are fabricated. People do not really live according to type. Indeed, they could not live that way. The images that other people hold about me are infinite, as are the number of cuts I would make in exploring other people or myself. And so just as in reality we never fully know ourselves, so too we do not fully know other people. Yet amid such ignorance we embrace each other within the structure of society and are not alone.

A novelist tries to express reality as it is, without any trace of scissor cuts. Or at least he tries to wield the scissors so as to simulate a multiplicity of cuts that would seem to represent reality as it is. And so events, ideas, and characters must not be defined and molded to possess a single, static shape. The author should create as though he were reflecting the lives of others, when in fact each fictional character is holding up a mirror at different angles to the light. Gide makes an interesting remark in the "The Diary to *The Counterfeiters*": "It is essential to realize that one can only observe a person who is walking away, from behind." What, then, of the author's own mirror? To say that writers depict characters as though these characters were reflecting each other, each character possessing his own mirror, is to say that characters are not portrayed through the mirror of a single author. What are we to make of the mirror held up by a writer whose idea it is to control the overall structure of his fiction? Must this mirror inevitably reveal but a single cut?

Here Gide invented a device. He had a novelist, Edouard, who was writing a book similarly titled "The Diary to *The Counterfeiters*," appear as the hero of the novel. And he let Edouard have his own mirror. Then, because he was standing about idly while his form was being reflected, Gide wrote "The Diary of a Counterfeiter," where he records the quotidian sensations and emotions of the author during the actual creation of the novel. In other words, he sets up his own mirror opposite Edouard's. This is a device by which the author disappears, and only the novel itself remains. By way of this device, the reader is brought into contact with an imagined reality in its purest form. Gide's notion of a pure novel is to be found here, along with the significance behind his ironic remark that "one cannot imagine a novel purer than Mérimée's *Double Mepris*." This book, Mérimée's masterpiece, unfolds as though all artifice were invisible to the eye of the reader. There is no display of sensual charm, irony, or wit for the reader to stumble over. There is no face of the author, no depiction of a powerful passion or idea to pressure the reader. And so the reader is startled to encounter the pure expression of a strange human relationship. What we call purity is really a standard, the most radical standard, by which we might judge any form of art. All literature longs for purity. Moreover, when we speak of what constitutes purity, there is no reason to be stubbornly vague or obscure. Gide is a relativist to the extreme, and he invented the term "pure novel" simply because he believed purity to be a standard, more appropriate than truth or reality, by which to judge the quality of fiction. Still, what is valuable is not the concept of a pure novel but its spiritual form—the actual process of Gide's artistry—which led him perforce toward the concept of a pure novel while living amid the social uncertainties of the modern age.

In his "Essay on the Pure Novel," Yokomitsu Riichi notes that the two elements essential to popular fiction are chance and sentimentality. But were we to look at reality without blinders, surely we would witness the spectacle of people living just because of such things as chance and sentimentality. The authors of pure literature in our country, Yokomitsu observes, are bound instead to

concepts such as truth or necessity. Although they seem preoccupied with an objective reality, in fact they have entered a world of
deformity and abstraction.

To say that popular writers aim for a mass readership is to imply
that readers themselves are looking for a fictional summary of the
reality that daily surrounds them. For this reason, successful popular writing will exercise a certain restraint, depicting chance and
sentimentality only to the degree that it will not offend the reader's
common sense. The reader will not abide any chance or sentiment
that does not ring true. Of course the real world is filled to overflowing with the sort of chance or sentiment that no one wants to
acknowledge. If the popular writer were to cast his eye on such a
world, he would be at a loss over how to write. And so the chance
or sentiment that appears in the work of a Dostoevsky, for whom an
overflowing world was always the foundation of realism, is not related to the chance and sentiment portrayed in popular fiction. Yokomitsu's explanation—that *Crime and Punishment* is a pure
novel though it works like popular fiction—is just rhetoric, albeit
rhetoric of a dangerous kind. Surely it begs other issues; namely,
that a novel of such greatness would be valued by a reader who can
grasp only its popular elements; that our pure literature today is so
tedious that we find Yokomitsu resorting to such rhetoric to explain this Russian novel.

In Dostoevsky's writing, we repeatedly encounter certain sudden or accidental movements of the passions or of ideas that strike
us as being bizarre. We are struck this way because such things occur everywhere in real life, but not in popular fiction. The shape of
authentic accident or chance never appears in such writing. Instead, popular fiction is full of apparent coincidences, that is,
chance based not on life but on plot structure. Dostoevsky too was
compelled to make use of these formal, apparent coincidences as a
way to project his vision of a chance-filled reality. But he did this
because chance was a necessity for his method of creation.

Dostoevsky's work is replete with the sense that in this world
full of chance and sentiment, everything is relative. And the foundation of his realism was a persistent loyalty to this bewildering
reality. As a writer, Gide is more limited than Dostoevsky, yet he
engages the same reality, perhaps more self-consciously, and strug-

gles to render it in its purest shape, no scissor cuts applied to it: "And the subject of the book, if you must have one, is precisely that struggle between what reality offers him and what he himself intends to make of it." This is what he was hoping to realize in his pure novel. As I noted earlier, his was laboratory work. What he discovered was a device, a sort of regulator balancing the intake of the social and the individual into fiction. By means of this mechanism, Gide came to recognize the shape, the actual form, of his second self. This work has taken forty years and now exhibits the clearest, most elegant structure in all the modern fiction of the self.

4

"A writer's secret is not something he should talk about. However, come the time when he must reveal it, a new arena for modern writers will be created." Yokomitsu added these words to his recent essay collection. Indeed, they might be seen as the proper prologue to the collection. All our young writers seem to be troubled by the issues raised here. What intrigues me, however, is the psychological shadow of Yokomitsu that shrouds these words, the ambiguity of his language. What is this "writer's secret"? Why shouldn't the writer speak about it? Again, when must he speak about it? All this ambiguity, emerging even in an appended commentary, can be said to lie at the heart of the complications that exist in all of Yokomitsu's essays. How trying a task it is to deal with this ambiguity.

What is the writer's secret? At bottom, such a question points to goings-on "backstage," matters the writer need not reveal to the reader. To the Naturalists, who took it as an article of faith that art imitated Nature, issues of style were not worthy of being addressed, because no amount of concern with the correct style of expression could influence their unwavering belief in the limpid materiality of Nature. As a further example, in their "environment of feeling" [shinkyō] phase, our recent authors of watakushi shōsetsu sought to expose the intricate shadows of their personal lives and to dramatize for the reader its secrets. But being conscious neither of the difference between a personal and a social life nor of the essential gap between sensibility and expression, they were oblivious to questions of artistic technique or style. And so the fictional stage was set. It was to become the place for backstage talk. And this talk filled the writer and gave him a capacity for expression. Such enabling conditions form the basis for any healthy literature. But the health and happiness of personal fiction did not long survive. The writer's secret place had shifted.

The question of whether a writer should reveal his secret is tied to that of whether the secret itself might be the proper subject of writing. Authors may not really choose what they write about, nor do they imagine that their way of writing itself might become the subject of their work. Yet such unimagined things regularly occur. It is the case that writers are controlled in the very process of writing—their style becomes the subject of their work—and so they must create literature of a specific kind. What provides the truly essential material is not reality but a way of seeing reality, or a way of thinking about it. Given this understanding, there should no longer be any question as to whether an author should reveal his secret or not.

Gide is an author who has ambitiously constructed the "new arena" Yokomitsu refers to, and who has performed within it. The emergence of this adventurer, who appears to have suffered from a fin de siècle illness, is comprehensible if we recall the long tradition of French realism. And so a real question emerges: What enabling force, by way of his example or instruction, did Gide bring to Japanese writing?

Social customs are strange, but it is all the more strange to realize that where such customs do not exist, what we call literary reality is unthinkable. The issue is not one of a tradition being good or bad. I would say that it wholly exceeds our ability as writers to analyze the power that these traditions actually exert upon us. In a given social context, if the events a writer makes use of are alive, then even should he add nothing to them, a sympathetic chord will be struck in the reader's heart. To the fascination inherent in the literary treatment of such events, what could the writer possibly add by his new way of seeing or thinking about them?

This is an issue that has disturbed me for some time, and not only with regard to the content of fiction. A single word can be thought of in these terms. Because both content and diction have various ranges of density, a given word will seem richer to the degree that it belongs to history and society. A neologism, no matter how clever its invention, will not possess the fascination of a word that has endured, stained with the sweat and blood of generations. No matter how gifted the poet, if he strings together weightless words, he will not charm his audience. Speaking either narrowly about diction or more broadly about language in general, we might question how our young writers today hope to grasp some new literary reality, even as our traditions and social customs are collapsing everywhere around us.

Kawakami Tetsutarō has written an especially penetrating analysis of Yokomitsu's story "Flowers" that I would like to cite in part here:

> This work is really a caricature of modern youth and its complicated love life. The story appears to be a simple one, in the sense that love is universal, a staple both of traditional tales and contemporary popular writing. And yet love for Yokomitsu's modern youth is different. They are not inflamed with the passion of the romantic youth of a previous generation, nor do they luxuriate in the chic romances of the ultra-modern. They are simply children of good families, cultivated in all that represents modern culture. They are knowledgeable. They know that there is in love an element of physical desire, and equally, how foolish and troublesome an activity love has been over the course of human history. At the same time, they acknowledge the centrality of love for the life of the feelings and do not forget to gauge the effects of love upon everything from the most instinctual to the most frivolous or utilitarian aspects of real life. Moreover, through love they have come at last to participate in jousts of emotional superiority, entering them with an almost chivalric intensity. In a word, they do not love, but love the strategies of love.

This "love" is a great nuisance. But at least its complications are to be found in every quarter. Even in today's popular writing, where we shouldn't expect complications, a once central theme—the treasure that is love—has lost shape and definition. Readers of popular novels find in such writing what is ever new in their lives. And popular writers know that their audience is always looking for an updated *Konjiki yasha* (The demon gold) or *Hototogisu* (The cuckoo). Yet our contemporary popular writers cannot produce

what they know their audience requires. The love of modern bourgeois youth is too abrupt and random, too chance-filled, for the
written page. And so the writer must invent a story about a type of
love that did not exist in the past, does not exist now, and perhaps
never will exist. I often imagine that something of interest will
come of this, although it is foolish to think so, because such writing would require the collusion of readers looking for rank fabrication. Also, this type of love story would not be compelling to those
who have actually experienced love, no matter what their degree of
cultural sophistication.

And so to depict love and arouse the illusions of the multitude,
popular writers understand that an expressive formula like the Edo
romance is absolutely necessary. To be sure, our artists face formidable pressures to identify themes that are in some way contemporary. But the fact that period films and popular romances set in
the past are produced and elicit such remarkable audience response
is proof of how much residual feudal sentiment still exists in Japan.

Of course this sentiment operates alongside an aesthetic sensibility refined and nurtured by a deep cultural past. Such a sensibility detects the superficiality and randomness of feelings as they are
portrayed in Japanese films based on modern life. Although we all
realize that the *giri-ninjō* formula of desire versus duty in a period
piece is exceedingly remote from the terms of modern reality, we
also detect a certain elegance in its style and its representation of
actions and passions that are truly comprehensible, emerging as
they do from a clearly delineated social milieu. It may as well be
asked why Western films about modern life, as compared to our
gendaimono, enjoy such extraordinary favor among the intelligentsia? The reason is simple. Given our traditions and aesthetic
sensibility, we recognize in Western films a purer form of cultural
literacy. We sense, too, how awkward is our attempt to culturally
inscribe the look of a modern bar or the Ginza. Why do recordings
of the [Western] classics sell at an incomparably greater rate than
recordings of jazz? The issue turns not on the depth of our understanding of Western music, but on the plain fact that our ears detect
many more pure sounds in classical music. I feel the eyes and ears
of a people imbued with a long tradition, with a culture grown to

maturity in the past, are indeed marvelous things. I cannot doubt what my eyes see or my ears hear.

What sort of person would read Yokomitsu's "Flowers"? Are its sales low because it is too highbrow? But then Gide's *Narrow Gate* is a highbrow novel on the theme of modern love, and, in the Ya-mauchi translation, has been reprinted several times. By now it has perhaps outsold even some bestselling popular novels. What is so fascinating about Gide's book? What has so touched the feelings of young readers, oblivious no doubt to Gide's conscious literary intentions? Why did my wife, whose literary qualifications are of no special order, read Maupassant's *A Woman's Life* with such emotion? Readers are attracted to the splendid character and purity of the work, not to its traces of the popular. I have heard of Kawabata's recent remark: "The enemy of pure literature today is not popular writing, but the Iwanami Bunko series of translations." It may have been said in jest, but it is far more penetrating than the average intellectual's literary theory.

The intellectual is said to have a pale face. Yet our writers cannot easily depict this paleness. How are a band of anemic nihilists, who have lost every trace of a distinctive psychology and character, to be made into fictionalized heroes? With life confronting them in various strange guises, writers have found it increasingly difficult to fall back on the charm of familiar themes and old stories. As an objective reality has become by degrees harder to represent, writers turned inevitably to the subjective, to a reliance on personal ways of seeing and thinking. It was at such a juncture that Gide's style arrived and so fascinated our literati. Yet no one has since emerged to commit himself heart and soul to the literary consequences of this fascination. This is because our writers were not fully prepared for Gide.

Existing at a point beyond faith in representational or confessional literature, bounded by a belief in writing whose central focus would be the abstract world of self-consciousness, or in a type of blank writing that could scarcely be called a literary style, the new arena built by Gide to grasp a new literary reality was a structure Japanese writers could not easily comprehend. In terms of external, economic conditions, the contours of our social life continued

changing at an accelerated pace. Yet the sense of tradition embraced by our writers could not be expected to change so quickly.
Surely they were aware of the unrest and instability of the modern
world, while persisting in their fidelity to a representational or a
confessional writing style. Owing to their situation, wherein they
had inherited a *watakushi shōsetsu* totally innocent of ideological
strife, they lacked the power to conceptualize the impasse between
the individual and society or the issue of the self in flight from the
instability of life. Moreover, they had no conviction that literature
could be generated by the sheer power of ideas. And so at the beginning of the movement known as Neo-Perceptionism (it does seems
presumptuous to call such a thing a "movement"), there was a
wish to stabilize real life by means of a fresh technique, or to pret-
tify it with a newfound sensibility. This Neo-Perceptionist style
might be seen as the final metamorphosis of the *watakushi shōsetsu.*

While the "new" Western literature of Gide, Proust, and Joyce
was being introduced, it happened that Gide, whose fiction was
technically the least accomplished though the most provoking of
literary questions, was removed to one side. Moreover, no one of
intellectual daring emerged to explore a type of self-despair that
had generated the productive and highly acclaimed psychological
methods of Proust and Joyce. This further demonstrates the perdur-
ance of our naive belief in a literature of confessional realism. It
was difficult for our writers to build a new arena outside of or prior
to such a literary disposition. It was a truly forbidding task for Yokomitsu, whose style was deductive and highly ornate, to assimi-
late Gide's spare, inductive method. And so the tortuous, confessional turns of Yokomitsu's language derive from an ambivalence
that was unavoidable if any new arena were to be built.

We witness here the spectacle of a Japanese writer who wanders
through a tangle of methods, plans, and proclamations, not at all
timidly but, on the contrary, ever keen and even voracious in his
hunt for new foreign designs. It is symbolic of the difficulty our
modern literature has encountered since the day of its birth. Inevitably, a writer like Yokomitsu has become the subject of both unwarranted skepticism and unwarranted praise.

It is well known that Marxist writing first appeared on the Japanese literary scene at the turn of this century, or simultaneously with the arrival of a literature of individualism. Marxist thinking gave an indissolubly absolute color to the styles of individual writers, making it impossible for proletarian writing to exhibit any frivolous, merely decorative traits. Its prohibition against frivolity led to a certain impoverishment of literary style. Although it is quite possible to conceive of a stylistic theory that prohibits frivolity, it would be based on an assumption that beyond any social or individual experience lies a certain fixed human nature or human psychology. Most intellectuals who took up Marxist theory were unaware of its inherent assumptions or defects, even though when they set out to write, they faced people who were by degrees losing their fixed human nature or psychology amid the chaos of modernity. This illustrates how captivating and persuasive was the force of Marxist theory. Consequently, attention to style diminished, and the *watakushi shōsetsu* died. But what the ideologues vanquished was our *watakushi shōsetsu*, not a real literature of individualism of a kind that could have entered Japan along with Marxist writing.

In the aftermath of our recent *tenkō* controversy, it is too soon to tell what type of literature our writers will produce. No doubt this is a moment of crisis. Now, faced with the concrete task of writing, our writers must find out whether, and under what conditions, they might outlive the unfeeling ideology that they had once believed. The time has come for writers again to engage the problem posed by the self. Will they come to believe that an unvanquished "I" still exists within them? Where fiction writing is concerned, I am a bystander and cannot say that we will witness a movement toward an activist literature, such as was triggered by Gide's own *tenkō* affair. Have any of our proletarian authors read Gide with devotion or tracked his forty-year struggle for expression?

The *watakushi shōsetsu* may have died, but have we really disposed of the self? Perhaps the *watakushi shōsetsu* will appear again in a different form. Such is the possibility, so long as Flaubert's famous equation—"Madame Bovary, c'est moi"—remains in force.

MISCELLANEOUS WRITINGS: EXCERPTS

"One Brain"

(An early short story; June 1924)

It was three years ago, shortly after father died. My mother coughed blood. This sign of her illness, together with my own wretched nerves, my affair with a certain woman, the material poverty of our household—all this left me drained. In time I came to feel that I would write about those days. But as I began to write, I was stunned. I could see nothing clearly. My every attempt failed as I became increasingly enraged by my own fictional persona, cut off from the outside world, acting out a staged melancholy. And no sooner did I complete fictional fragments based on such whirling dreams, dreams only I could interpret, than I destroyed them.

"Recollections of Nakahara Chūya"

(August 1949)

To a painful degree, his poems were bound to his life. Trying to smile, his mouth twisted; trying to sing, his poem decayed. There is nothing here of the harmony of poetic creation. Just as Nakahara the man clashed with human nature, as a poet he clashed with poetry. Rather than call him a poet, we should call him a confessionalist. He loved Verlaine, but it seems he was saying that before all else, Verlaine desired music and, with it, confession. Nakahara himself showed no concern either for the musical or the structural characteristics of poetry. He did not exercise his mind and heart over such things as the intellectual structure of art. That is, he did not question the process whereby the poet himself creates language in a poem, if only after exploring how his own words—words already existing in history and society, possessing colors and a density not easily altered for all the artistry of the poet—might possibly survive on their own. He did not have the leisure for such complications. What was important to him was the act of confession, not the construction of a poem. He seemed to think that language, any and all language, welled up from within. And so his poetics were essentially an ethics.

"Rimbaud I," "Rimbaud II," "Rimbaud III"
(October 1926; February 1930; March 1947)

Here, after all, we encounter the phenomenon, Rimbaud. This Rimbaud, who committed literary suicide at nineteen, did not have the soul of an artist. He had a merchant's spirit. For Rimbaud, making a poem was equivalent to trafficking in ivory. Yet such reasoning is empty before the work itself. We must not obscure the mysterious power of his masterwork, *A Season in Hell*, which might have been lost had he continued to write poetry. In that poem, he rudely threw open the door on taboo and hauled out his destiny. He once remarked: "Wanting to die, I summoned my executioners, to bite the barrel of their guns." He did not simply observe his muse in flight from within the safe passivity of self-consciousness. He captured his muse, and they stabbed each other. Truly, his is a literature of excess.

. . .

No writer spoke of himself like Rimbaud. He never stammered. Savagely he confessed, and the confession itself became a silvery song. Even his dug-up mud glistens. His language was always bodily, his own marvelous flesh. The gentlest of his passages are lined with steel muscle. No author so ignored the reader as did Rimbaud. He sang neither for the chosen nor even for himself. To escape from song, he broke the songs that surfaced and threw the pieces away.

. . .

99

My first encounter with Rimbaud came by accident. I was twenty-three, it was springtime, and I was on a leisurely stroll through Kanda. Suddenly a stranger, coming the other way, knocked me down. I was caught completely offguard. Not even in my dreams did I imagine how powerful an explosive charge had been set inside that shabby, compact volume of *A Season in Hell*— the Mercure edition—which unexpectedly caught my eye in the shopwindow of a certain bookseller. Moreover, the firing mechanism for this explosive was so sensitive that my own dubious linguistic powers were scarcely questioned. This small book exploded in the most marvelous way, so that years later I still remain in the vortex of the event "Rimbaud." I certainly feel it to be an event. How others see the matter I do not know, but at least for me, literature, a single literary idea, theme, or expression, is an actual event. And I believe I first learned this from Rimbaud.

. . .

It should be seen first of all that the instability of Rimbaud's poetic forms does not derive from any ambiguity about his subject, but from his strict observation of specific things.

. . .

In modern poetry, the Romantic movement was already at an end, although it left behind a dark and massive wound in its denial of material reality. And no one knew when the dawn would come because poets of every fashion and school just played with the wound. Suddenly, in the distant sky appeared a burning star and a voice that cried, "Open your eyes." With the dawn, a child fell among standing trees. Rimbaud, for the sake of poetry, re-embraced the concrete materiality of the world, whose existence could no longer be denied.

. . .

That strange materialist Rimbaud put no faith in anything subjective. Lyrical poetry held not the slightest attraction for him. All the powers of his concentration were always directed at the material world and at the tip of our senses that touch it.

"The Muse and the Fate of Akutagawa Ryūnosuke"

(October 1927)

As a student, I was an enthusiastic reader of the works of Akutagawa. At the time he committed suicide, I was still in college and wrote an essay about him that had the same title as this one. Now it is lost somewhere, but it was my earliest criticism. I do not remember very well the substance of what I wrote, although I do recall having been inordinately taken with Chesterton's essay on George Bernard Shaw, and that I wrote my piece on Akutagawa with it very much in mind. I had no feeling of sympathy for his suicide. I felt, rather, that his skepticism should have taken him much further. Akutagawa clung stubbornly to the intellectualism of Gourmont and Anatole France, whom he evidently loved. But I thought he should have had a more vital and intense, a higher-speed intellectualism. Since that time, I have not re-read Akutagawa's work. Were I to read him again today, how would I react? Perhaps I would be surprised and discover in Akutagawa a traditional Japanese poet.

"An Approach to *Flowers of Evil*"

(November 1927)

Radical forgetfulness is but another form of radical hope. It marks the destiny of the soul that, having received life, wishes to see no end to it. It was Baudelaire's genius to have captured a world-weariness that is itself an expression of this radical hope. Despite his ennui, he cherished memories of a distant past, a place in the stream of time, the very day on which the soul and body went separate ways. One person seeks consciousness and lives. Another seeks sleep and dies. Baudelaire yearned to gaze upon his own, other self.

The ennui that encircled Baudelaire is not at all a monotony. It generates a radical tension. It distinguishes the soul's incarnation from the surrounding death of reality. It signifies the most humble form of human passion. The soul dreams to the beat of the human heart. But we can no longer speak of this merely as a state of mind. What I see before me is the hushed figure of a poet, walking the stone streets of Paris.

Here, provisionally, we give the name "ennui" to a condition that may well contain the seeds of all creation, although it does not itself signify creation. To be sure, ennui is an absolute, and for us an absolute should call to mind a Nirvana rejecting all human action. But creation is an action, the most human sport of all. In that sense, Christ's vision of God was an absolute; it was not a creation. Yet even though Christ had an absolute vision of God, he himself could move only one step at a time. He had to transform this absolute into an action of the body and the blood. Creation exists not for truth, or for beauty, or because of a transcendental command. It is but one kind of necessity, like fruit that must fall from a tree.

"Shiga Naoya" and
"A Study of Shiga Naoya"
(December 1929; February 1938)

Shiga is a man neither of thought nor of sensibility, but of action in all things. His soul is the soul of a doer. All the talent he possesses has not the slightest meaning outside the context of real life. For Shiga, literary creation is an integral part of real life, and so it is natural that it would be steeped in actuality. It is natural, too, that art would emerge not after a separation from real life but as a distillation of it.

. . .

Shiga's work is of the humblest kind, impervious to the issue of his wealth and leisure. He is saving his life through literature.

. . .

The realism of Shiga Naoya is always under the sway of the author's intensity. To put it another way, his realism is bursting with a poetry distinctive to him. The other day, during a *zadankai* with Shiga, Takii Kōsaku made what may seem a bizarre observation, although I caught what he intended. He said that within the tradition of Japanese poetry, there are no lyrics to be found, at least among those poems of the highest distinction. This is as true of *Man'yōshū* poems as of those that mark [Matsuo] Bashō's true style. What we have in them is not lyricism but realism. It may seem that nature is ever in view, when in fact a curtain shrouds it. It is only when this curtain is deftly raised that something comes clear, say, a mountain, or a bird, or a wristwatch, some element of existence that we can now, unmistakably, see. And what reveals this is poetry. Poetry is a song that bursts forth from within.

If we are certain that in *waka* or *haiku* a tradition of rules governing poetic expression runs deep and strong, then in the light of this tradition, Shiga's realism appears extremely poetic. Among our contemporary authors of the first rank, Shiga's technique may be the simplest. In a sense, it could even be called impoverished. Yet the strength and purity of its character are virtually without peer. This cannot be called elegance; rather, it is a style that turns a marvelously clear, serene eye on anything vital and alive.

Of course techniques of realism made advances under the influence of scientific progress. And just as in science, where reality is exposed and dissected into a variety of elements, so too in realist writing, the world is spread out to be analyzed by a basic, elemental language. Of course to be prey to such a delusion regarding culture and the world signals either an unconscious abuse of science or else a careless fantasy.

The victory of mechanization in the modern novel rests on such a delusion. Be it psychology, emotion, character, or action, everything is converted into material elements that construct human beings. And the predisposition to classify all these elements so as to build the world of the novel has in consequence killed off the poet in the writer. To produce correct observations, the writer has sacrificed the poet who dwells within. How can we possibly trust observations produced in this way?

To speak of a realism that has lost its poetry is to speak of a loss of style because of excessive faith in what is called non-subjective observation. What after all are these "observations," carried out by writers who possess no distinctive style? Who would have ever expected this of literature? Yet this loss of style is the unmistakable characteristic of modern writing. Because realism never encountered resistance from a writer's style, it flooded the scene with great force. Writers were rendered totally passive and just luxuriated in the omnipotence of a realism prepared to represent all that was out there to be observed. If some difficulty arose in representation, it was dismissed as some sort of external obstacle, such as political censorship. But so long as such obstacles did not exist, writers were led by realism every which way. This is the destiny conferred by a bad strain of realism.

People speak of the beauty of Shiga's portrayals of nature. This beauty could only be expressed by a writer for whom observation and feeling are conjoined in a single action. For a certain observed fact to take on an unalterable, unique reality, it must be dyed in the color of the feelings a single observer experienced at a specific place and time. This is a healthy, human experience, one that leads to the discovery of narrative poetry. Flaubert knew this very well, as he revealed in his remark "In all the world, no two trees or stones are alike." But it takes a strong will to safeguard the truth of this maxim, something lost to our degenerate realists.

· · ·

The heart of a child who never forgets the name of a character in a story is directly in touch with the wisdom of history, which preserves any number of human types as they emerge over the centuries in stories and novels.

· · ·

Whatever else it may be, love is an action, an act of will. It does not simply exist. Rather, it is something that human beings discover, invent, and protect. Therefore, the beauty and the truth of a great love novel will be grounded, without exception, on the vow made between a man and a woman, a vow to make their joy real and actual. It is from this that *Anya kōro* (A dark night's passing) derives its strong, ethical tone.

· · ·

To modern intellectuals, nothing seems more alien than the word "happiness." They no longer consider that their unhappiness might be of their own making and have abandoned the courage it would take to recreate happiness by and for oneself. I have no intention to counter this stubborn, general current in the air of our time. There is nothing that can be done. For that very reason, it is a "general current." Now, for any new idea to be born, it is usually the case that the general current of the time comes to be seen as a material stumbling block. In the past, it has been the *moraliste* who has raised the most serious objection to ideas being given such material reality. And this has not changed since the days of Montaigne.

. . .

Shiga does not play the verbal games beloved of our modern literati, whereby anxieties are translated into words that are in turn
stumbled over. His sufferings come straight from life without such
verbal mediation. To achieve this reversal, Shiga used nothing
other than the wisdom of a person who knows life by living it; in
other words, he has used nothing other than a real power of spirit.

※※

"On Theory and Practice"
(April, May, July 1930)

   This is my first monthly book review assignment. "Could you
lend me all your copies of this month's literary magazines," I asked
Kawabata Yasunari recently. He burst into laughter, saying, "At
last, they've turned to a real know-nothing. . . ." It is true; I have
nothing to offer by way of defense. But I should describe my recent
mood, which is one of unremitting discontent, as I stare at this
monstrous accumulation: "agit-prop demands," "dialectical materialist perspective," "the hegemony of the literary world," and so
many other new coinages, fabricated from the arrogance of a gang
of literary critics.

. . .

   What I find disgusting in this book is all the jargon pushing this
or that "ism," this or that "school," and inflicting on the reader who
wishes to comprehend the book's argument a prior belief in this jargon. As I indicated earlier, I don't trust jargon. In fact, I believe that
not trusting jargon is the mark of critical spirit.

. . .

   It is truly dismaying to see how our youthful contributors to the
literary arts glare jaundice-eyed at each other as they declare themselves members of "the proletarian school," "the aesthetic school,"
and so forth. Who could possibly know whether one possesses a
proletarian or a bourgeois nature? I possess just the poor trappings

of my self-consciousness and am satisfied to voice what I really feel.

. . .

Miki Kiyoshi observes that there is no such thing as a pure artistic sensibility. This is most certainly true, just as in this world no pure water flows. Beyond any human capacity to describe it as pure, artistic sensibility exists in defiance of neat prescriptions. It is said also that there can be no sensibility or human will that is not socially and historically circumscribed. This too is obvious. And although one's sensibility or will can be shaped by social and historical circumstance, it is not at all affected by any scholar's theory.

. . .

Just as certain social conditions produce material known as commodities in the world, so too are literary works produced by a natural process of the human spirit. As products of language, they are not in the least bit different from sheer material objects. But just as commodities in and of themselves have no meaning, so too is language in and of itself meaningless. Meaning emerges at the point of human exchange. It is surpassingly simple to draw an analogy between the magical qualities that commodities assume upon exchange, and the magical qualities that language takes on in any discourse. The theory of dialectical materialism in our day has recorded numerous such triumphs. But it has yet to lay a single finger on the basic character of language. This is a fact that critics must admit to and analyze dispassionately.

. . .

I frequently hear odd complaints that my criticism is difficult, although I don't recall ever having set forth a difficult argument. In fact, I cannot recall having discussed theory, except to say that difficult theories are rather frivolous ornaments. For argument's sake, if on occasion my criticism seems difficult, it can be for one of two reasons, and no other. Either it is because my method of expression is clumsy; or because it is a far more difficult task to speak of simple facts than to discuss complex theories.

. . .

Whether a given critical essay is logically correct or incorrect is not an important issue. Always the more difficult question is whether an argument moves people or leaves them unmoved. If one were to look closely at the specifics of Mr. Yokomitsu's essay, it would be easy to uncover a number of mistakes. But the fact that the style of the piece seems like a scattershot attack on everything is owing solely to the author's sincere, and seasoned, passion.

"Is Literature Unreal?"

(September 1930)

One could call Masamune Hakuchō a Naturalist, which would tell us nothing about his spirit as a writer. The Naturalist writer Flaubert was a martyr to his dreams of sculptural beauty. Zola was bewitched by the phantom of social justice. No matter how objectively written a novel, truly great fiction shines with a double vision: the vision of characters in the novel and the author's vision. Perhaps it exceeds our power to capture clearly the vision of the author, but if we do not even try to close in and grasp it, criticism degenerates into an array of futile catchwords and slogans.

. . .

There is nothing more pitiful than being stuck for cigarette money after buying a stupid book.

"Yokomitsu Riichi"
(November 1930)

The world is a machine possessing many dark, unfathomable components. There is nothing beyond this machine. Convictions of this kind are found at the core of some of our finest novelists. We might say that in the heart of a novelist lies a terrible taste for such grand if desolate facts about existence. As far as possible, the novelist conceals his own shape. He believes in no system of thought but what he sees in the mechanism of the world. The thoughts expressed by the novel's characters are simply the thoughts of novelistic characters. It is quite redundant, then, for novelists to use the word "machine" in their titles. It is but a figure of speech. Yet the case of Mr. Yokomitsu's "Kikai" (Machine) is totally different. In this story, the term "machine" maintains a pure, symbolic meaning in the author's heart.

The characters in this story function like machines that have been welded to the structure of the nameplate factory. This in itself is not so important. What is crucial is that the character in the work referred to as "I" speaks from a full recognition of these machine functions. Of course the author is greater than this "I." However, the philosophy of this "I" is the philosophy of the author. The author of this work is not straining in the least for a new way of grasping human psychology or for a revolution in fictional style. He is narrating instead how a writer arrives at what he believes.

. . .

"Machine" is not an ode to belief, but to sincerity. The authentic shape of human sincerity is achingly depicted here. The author portrays sincerity drawn out to its fullest extreme. But note that this is not what the world calls being sincere.

"A Passion for Materiality"

(December 1930)

It is a very rare experience for me to be moved by a poem or a song that sings of the streams and mountains or that sings in faint sighs; in other words, by poems far removed from the baseness of this floating world. Yet there are moments when such a modest and refined human perspective yields unexpected clarity on the structure of reality, and this can be startling. The poet is not a placid type who composes odes to beauty. Reality is simply what exists, and the poet is someone who must rely on beauty to close in on reality. In that sense, beauty is as fully necessary to the poet as passion is to a man who would move toward the woman he loves.

. . .

Our writers have tried various ways to depict the modern metropolis, even though already the city has lost its character. All these metropolitan marches—what preposterous nonsense. So much of our writing is set in bars and dance halls. This is not a literature of those who have lived in a city, but of stupefied bumpkins gone sight-seeing.

"Marx's Insight"
(January 1931)

As Marx observed to Rugé, "The problem is confession, only that. To obtain forgiveness for their sins, human beings must confess their sins as they are."

Correspondingly, objective theory is just a confession of things as they are. . . . Here lies the core issue regarding theory and practice. To turn the theory of dialectical materialism into flesh and blood, it does not take tortuous reasoning, only effort. It is scholarly nonsense to claim that theory and practice are dialectically united at their origin, as if theory and practice were the same thing. Marx did not propagate the dialectical unity of theory and practice, but enacted it in his life.

. . .

What will come of lamenting the inadequacy of standards based on class struggle, or of escapist grasping for the sleeve of the muse in flight? Beauty is a reality as bitter as the class struggle.

"Disqualified as a Critic"
(February 1931)

The single most distinctive feature of literary criticism in modern Japan, what must be said before anything else, is that raw intellect contributes nothing to it. It is all just a matter of dulled nerves producing theory.

· · ·

No criticism will emerge from the proposition that art must be seen as a holy object, somehow transcending real life.

· · ·

Try to imagine a society equipped with a single language that followed pure logic. It would be totally deranged. People have no capacity—beyond derangement—for truly understanding the language that they use. And for that very reason there is sure to exist inside every mind a castle built of abhorrence toward a fixed and stable language.

"On the Work of Ibuse Masuji"
(February 1931)

While he is narrating his dream in "Koi" (Carp), Ibuse is not using any sort of technique. He is giving us a direct expression from
his heart. Yet he is not at all sentimental. As we read "Carp," we
simply feel the author's unsentimental heart. His heart possesses
nothing that could be described as sentiment but something of
much deeper significance—a vitality of the flesh, whose color the
story so marvelously captures.

If Ibuse's heart were sentimental, then both the protagonist, as
well as the carp thrown into the pool, would be sentimental. But
the author's sentiment, like that of a carp who does not know writing, is not given to pondering the possible meanings contained in
the letters that spell *sentiment*. A certain corporeal sorrow, as nar-
rated in "Carp," infuses all of the author's work. He opens this
small piece with the line: "For over ten years now, I have been obsessed with a single carp." Is the author still so obsessed? At any
rate, I believe this small "Carp" lies below all his creation.

His eyes are not those of a novelist but of a poet. Such eyes are
ever cast inward, yet what is glimpsed there is no psychological
strife, just a single white carp swimming. I think that Ibuse is honestly convinced that this living thing is a symbol of the sorrow in
his heart. And when he attempts to express this conviction, all of
reality becomes just a single white carp. Still, this conviction is
slippery. It would require an exceedingly powerful will to make

this white carp swim peacefully. Ibuse does not have this kind of strength. If he had it, he would be a different person, and a sense of anxiety would be part of this work. He has been obsessed by a carp for over ten years. Rather than moving toward broad knowledge of the world, he has come to be ridiculed for his narrow obsession. For that very reason, Ibuse's sorrow signifies both his sacrifice and his rebellion. That is, his sorrow is two layers deep. And I believe it is to express this double sorrow that his writing turns not into poetry but into fiction.

"The Psychological Novel"
(March 1931)

I once had occasion to write: "Psychology is like liquor that goes straight to your head. You say to yourself, 'My, my, wasn't that fine. Cheap too.' But later you pay for it. I've swilled more than my fair share of both." At the time, I didn't mean to be humorous. Although a branch of science, psychology is really a curious mixture of rhetoric and metaphysics, possessing a seductive charm that never fails to provoke anxiety. Did Janet have anything to teach Bourget? Did Proust learn anything from Freud? Or was it just the opposite?

"The Debate on the Scientific
Nature of Literary Criticism"
(April 1931)

For some time now there has been a great uproar over the issue
of the relative aesthetic or political value of art. Does art intrinsically possess more of one or the other? But really we ought to ask:
What good will come of speaking about art in terms of any "value"?
Why don't we just admit that an artwork possesses the autono-
mous value of its own origins, which is both the necessary and the
sufficient cause of the critic's activity? Why aren't we satisfied to
engage substantive issues, such as for what reason, to what degree,
and by what devices, a given work moves people. The reluctance to
do this is baffling. Art, from any angle, remains art. If it were something else, then it would be called by another name. Indeed, we
should invent another name. Artistic values, to the end, represent
the values of art. This much should be clear, unless of course we
choose deliberately to complicate the issue.

. . .

It is said that commodities in their true form were revealed by
Marx, but properly speaking what was revealed by a Marxist analysis of commodities was their social function. In other words, commodities first assume their true form at the moment it is made
clear that they actually embody production relations in society. For
Marx, what is called the "function" of commodities signifies at the
same time their existence. In this sense, as compared to the discussion of commodities in earlier economic theory, commodities

within Marxist economics appear to be a far more spiritual phenomenon. Why should people remain so obsessively attached to distinctions between spirit and matter, idealism and materialism, and so forth? Read the first chapter of the first book of *Capital*. How do we characterize the method Marx uses to so exhaustively investigate commodities? Idealist? Materialist? It is neither one nor the other.

"Tanizaki Jun'ichirō"

(May 1931)

As everyone knows, Poe loved the strange, the terrifying, the perverse. Tanizaki also loved these things. But Poe loved them precisely because he believed them to be true, to be elements of a reality truer and more authentic than the everyday world around him. In the background, always, soared his *Eureka* vision of the world. But Tanizaki's case was totally different. His affection for the abnormal was but a single facet of his sensibility, a taste, albeit one whose reality derived from being powerfully rooted in his character. For Poe, beauty existed as an absolute imperative of reason, whereas for Tanizaki, beauty was made necessary by his senses.

. . .

Tanizaki is an idealist. However, he is an idealist attached to the sensuous forms that are ever before his eyes, the actual feelings that occupy his heart; an idealist, then, for whom a carnal shock is an absolute necessity. At first glance, this seems contradictory. To unite apparent opposites—the ideal and the sensual—would seem to complicate the issue. But it is really quite straightforward. It seems complicated only to weak individuals who lack idealist or sensual power. A writer like Tanizaki who possesses a robust ego and submerges himself in carnal consciousness rejects all abstract ideas. He does not abide general observations about culture and society. The worldview of this instinctual idealist is not necessarily simple, but it is absolutely pure. For Tanizaki, the world is fully sufficient. Whether it leads to pleasure or to pain, the world always offers him sustenance in the form of distinct physiological sensations. Just so is the life of the body driven by desire. Here is the source of Tanizaki's aestheticism, which must be distinguished from the aestheticism of Wilde.

. . .

Tanizaki exposed devils, but not once did he reveal a so-called diabolism. His devils and heretics were not masks. In the main, devils and heretics originate in a rebellion against the world. However, Tanizaki's devils and heretics are born in submission to the world. They are, in essence, totally ignorant of the artistic attitude that sneers at the world, and are unable to resist any demand of the heart no matter how extreme.

"French Literature and the New Japanese Literature"

(July 1931)

In some recent issues of magazines as different from one another as *Shi to shiron* (Poetry and poetics), *Shi/Genjitsu* (Poetry/reality), and *Shin bungaku kenkyū* (New literary studies), it appears that most of the space is being used to introduce the new literature from abroad. In this effort, much French writing is being translated. The fiction of the great Proust, the intricate poetic theories of Valéry, the criticism of Gide, along with faithful translations of several long novels, have begun to appear. Yet I remain quite skeptical. I wonder if this literature of the first order, which requires immense perseverance even to comprehend superficially, will have any staying power in our frenetic literary world. I say this because the French writing is of an extremely solitary and personal nature, making it unthinkable of approach by any sort of random intellectual preparation. Rather, it can be approached only by a direct engagement of the work in one's own person and, at that, only after there has been an examination of the self. But in our present situation, critics surface and pass smug judgments on this literature, although they have never read it. So frenetic is our culture that foreign literature is despised before it is read.

"On Pure Fiction"

(December 1931)

Reading Tanizaki's essay, what struck me first was his obvious love for *Tsuyu no atosaki* (Before and after the rains) even as he was writing criticism about it. Through Tanizaki's style itself, I took in the palpable pleasure he had felt reading [Nagai] Kafū's work. How youthful and pliant was the pen that limned its impressions of this story. Of course Tanizaki is a writer of formidable literary cultivation and output. Yet his heart can still be moved to a fresh response. He goes out and embraces writing that others find hard to reach. Compared to the youthfulness of Tanizaki's style, what our young critics write today seems old and stodgy.

. . .

Now then, what did the pure eyes of Tanizaki see when they looked into Kafū's work? They saw the author's attitude as a writer; that is, they gazed into Kafū's own eyes.

"On Valéry"

(May 1932)

Intoxicated as I was on Baudelaire and Rimbaud, I did not find Valéry's poetry at all interesting. I recall too that when I began to read Mallarmé, I found even his poetry to be more intense. Instead, I fell headlong into Valéry's criticism. His essays completely crushed the notion I had held previously about what criticism is or could be. For the first time I experienced the vertigo induced by theory.

"On Paradox"

(June 1932)

Novelists ridicule, satirize, or deal ironically with human thoughts and actions, but people live by embracing far more incomprehensible things. It is obvious that with the help of ideas and theories, one can re-envision human life. We might also agree that in Japanese novels, human life always seems to exist beyond such re-envisioning. What is most lacking in the tradition of the Japanese novel is a certain intellectual, speculative disposition. If we regard ideas and theories as having real power and a de facto presence in the world, yet do not find them flourishing in the novel, in other words, in the literary form best suited to their flourishing, then quite naturally the novel will seem impoverished. Most of our writers, ignoring ideas and theories, have taken pleasure in depicting human life in all its incomprehensibility. This is not a pleasure predicated on the rejection of any idea or theory. Rather, it is a pleasure there from the beginning, in the nurturing of an anti-intellectual style.

. . .

At the heart of any real paradox, there must always be fierce, direct observation and intelligence sharp enough to perceive what exists beyond reason in real life. Paradox is not frivolous, but part of creation. It is the open expression of an analyst who faithfully pursues, himself in motion, a reality that is on the move.

"Fiction Studies, I"

(June 1932)

Film is an art of excess sensation. It is a scheme whereby hundreds of people are crammed inside a gloomy box and abandon their spirits to an electrical machine. We can observe two species of people at films: the first are rapturously paralyzed while inside the box; the second leave the box looking shamefaced and bewildered as they encounter the police stations and public toilets of the real world. This is more or less the anticipated effect of anything that goes by the name of art. But no other art takes it so far as does film.

. . .

They say that in an age of frayed nerves like our own, there is no proper interval for dreaming. However, no one claims that we are fully conscious. It is just that our dream-center has shifted from the human heart to the bewildering spectacle outside. As machine violence continues to agitate and alter our sense of form and movement in Nature, the lineaments of Nature gradually come to resemble a dream. At this point, a human, spiritual need to shape our own dreams fades away. Both the capacity and the patience to dream for oneself is lost. Yet the craving to dream remains. How convenient, then, for people to just go and stand dumbfounded in the city streets, where the high-speed, manufactured motion seems already dream-like.

. . .

I want to convey what was fundamentally at stake while the gap separating fact from fantasy lessened by degrees. When people come to live like automatons, leading a passive daily existence, listening only to gossip about strangers, it becomes more and more difficult to draw distinctions between language and fact. A man falls in love without even knowing the woman. He may be infatuated, but with the fiction of love. Such is the modern character.

"Letter to X"

(September 1932)

I hope to be faithful to the unique movements of my own sensibility. It may be more correct to say that I have been driven toward such faithfulness, quite literally driven. And to be driven in this sense is enough for me. I am convinced that to be faithful means to be driven, whatever else it may mean. And so I have come to look upon those who shamelessly use words like "faithfulness," "love," or "righteousness," as if for the quaint sounds of their syllables, with profound incomprehension.

. . .

All writing consists of tales and legends. Nothing factually reliable has ever been inscribed.

. . .

I cannot trust the ideology of individualism any more than I can believe in other blatant ideologies. The issue of belief or nonbelief notwithstanding, it is a fact that each of us lives by clinging to a sense that our own life experience cannot fully be described to another. Indeed, this is the actual condition of individuality. And this sense that one cannot convey one's own experience to another shapes a variety of attitudes, of one class toward another, of one century toward another. Perhaps our intellect is capable of giving order to these random complications. Yet it is inconceivable that we were given an intellect for the sole purpose of restoring any such order.

"Notebook II"

(March 1933)

Before all else, Gide and Valéry were critics. They were stubborn self-critics. It was never a significant issue, at least for them, whether the narration of their critical spirit took the form of a novel or a poem. Literature was but a medium to discover and establish the self. Moreover, they could not trust any medium but literature, which left them in a vulnerable position. Indeed, they shared a common tragedy, in being born writers whose deepest anxiety was over the question: What is literature?

And so it was natural that their characteristic assertion ("no question can be resolved before reducing it to a question of the self") pointed them toward pure literature or literary solitude and away from the rules of rhetoric, from conventional ideas, from formal theories, and, needless to say, from the commercialism of the world. Of course it is easy from our vantage to see them both as leading figures in the pure literature movement. But it was not easy for them, conscience-stricken as they were over the question of what kind of pure literature they desired. The extent of their discipline and training testifies to how difficult a task this was.

"On Literary Criticism"
(April 1933)

Ideas that possess no tradition are always abstract. Language that has forgotten tradition is always false.

People say: "Your criticism is poor because it is the criticism of bourgeois liberalism." But this reproach is only possible because of a complete obliviousness to the fact that modern bourgeois literary criticism in the West began with the sufferings of Sainte-Beuve, an event without parallel or connection to Japan. A bizarre situation has evolved whereby those reproached, who typically have not performed one act of anything like liberal criticism, flatter themselves the more by saying, "See. I stand accused. My criticism must be liberal after all."

I am not exaggerating. Within the critical world of modern Japan, we can witness countless such scenes of a complicated farce. But we need to examine the patients and not the pathology.

It was Valéry who once remarked that "criticism is simply the political element of literature." It is a wise statement so long as we read it without irony. I would like to paraphrase Valéry in trying to describe the state of our literary world: "Criticism is simply the literary element of politics."

"Tanizaki Jun'ichirō's *Primer on Style*"

(January 1935)

At first it seemed quite ordinary. But when I finished this *Primer* and reflected on it, I realized it was a masterpiece.

Intellectuals with literary aspirations have said that the book contains its share of embarrassments, or that it lacks novelty. I agree. The book could seem tedious if read in a certain way. After all, for writers obsessed with constructing the new literature, the issue is not how to write well but how to write correctly; or not even how to write correctly, but how to see or think correctly, the primary requirements being those of conviction and ideology. The problem of style is secondary. And so it is fashionable to believe that if one's convictions are high-minded, style will follow. In the face of the question—How are we to live?—there are serious people who claim that stylistic concerns should be held in abeyance. From here it degenerates into a noisy clamor over how to define realism. Meanwhile we live in a world where people can scarcely write a satisfactory letter, much less portray human character.

Although there is no ideology or conviction that does not issue from self-love, that is, from a place where language and style are freely shaped by the self, at the moment an ideology or conviction enters the world, there is resistance to its language and style, indeed a formidable resistance unimaginable so long as everything was thought to exist inside one's head. Generally speaking, a writer begins by trying to control language and proceeds to learn ways to

skillfully master it. This is as true in Japan as it is in foreign countries. It forms the basis for all treatises on style. Because Tanizaki's
essay is itself built on this foundation, we might call it his "record
of mastering a language of the spirit." This language represents
Tanizaki's maturity. It is meaningless to accuse it of being conservative, since essays on style are conservative by nature.

Tanizaki has explained that he intended this primer for a popular
audience, not as something to show literati or academics. Perhaps
because I am neither a *bunjin* nor an academic, I found much to
learn from it. The argument here may appeal to a popular audience,
but it contains not a single empty theory. And it is just this sort of
popular writing, full of practical advice, which is beyond the reach
of our mediocre literati and academics.

"More Thoughts on the Literary Review"
(March 1935)

I will not inflict my ambitions on the reader. Indeed, I feel no need to do so. Still, as critics, if we do not bring the joy of creation to our critical practice, no matter what that practice may be, we will experience no recovery from the real weakness of our contemporary literary world, now hidden behind its gaudy outward spectacle. For the fact is we have critical writings but no critics; critical methods but no critical spirit. Such are my thoughts on the matter.

"Yokomitsu Riichi's *Book of Remembrance*"

(June 1935)

Our emerging writers do not face any clear objects because they refuse to engage, as a matter of necessity, the secrets of their craft. For example, whether in their representations of love or of murder, what they portray is merely a love-like love, a murderish murder. We witness here a psychological flow, but nothing to grasp and hold onto. What we find are actions stripped of motivation. How is it possible to represent fictionally the existence, much less the loves, of men and women, when a sense of character has been lost? It may well be that the fictional landscape is full of passionate convictions, but in their depiction we see merely the strutting of disembodied theories. It isn't just that writers facing chaos lost all belief in the reality of the objects they portrayed. Rather, in trying to represent such chaos as part of the world, they understood the difficulty of capturing reality in literature. And, as a result of finding it hard to grasp the real shape of things, writers inclined toward their own subjectivity. Their concerns presently revolve around the question, not of what should be represented but of how one should represent it. Writers are thus driven toward a situation where "how one writes" goes far beyond a simple question of technique, indeed where it replaces in importance what one writes about. In other words, the very issue of how one writes becomes the object of representation.

"Face of the Author"
(January 1936)

I have no desire to look back on my past life and represent it. It isn't that I regard such effort as trivial. Quite simply, it is impossible. How could I set out now to trace my footsteps in the mud of times past? Those who are writing *watakushi shōsetsu* today are surely walking on sand. I believe that when he looks back on the self he once was, a man appears to be nothing. And so I feel only shame when I read such fiction, wherein this twice-removed demon is reproduced.

"Ideas and Real Life"
(April 1936)

No idea exists apart from real life. But only animals have ideas that do not necessitate some sacrifice of real life. The social order may be called real life but it represents just a sacrifice paid for by an idea. The relative texture of our real life is in direct proportion to the depth or the shallowness of some requisite sacrifice. It is in this context that the word "tradition" materializes. Of course, the same applies to the individual. Ideas are nurtured by the habitual sacrifice of real life. And the steady work that produces the reality of the social order, involving the cooperation of humanity over time, becomes all the more complex and difficult when, faced with a vital idea, it necessitates the active labor of an individual. The true thinker is rare. So long as we never encounter directly such a rare human being, we will be manipulated at will by ideas as if they were so many instruments used to classify or to dissect real life. In other words, we will be manipulated by an ideological force called abstraction.

Masamune Hakuchō has referred to "abstract thoughts that appear to us as ghosts." Too many people fear ghosts. Too many others have grown used to them.

"A Response to Nakano Shigeharu"

(April 1936)

You characterize me as someone consumed in the effort to unleash chaos on the language of criticism. I am seen to be an obstacle to literary progress, a producer of imbecilic epigones. You say that critics like me must be brought to heel. I will not say that you are not entitled to such grand pronouncements. Still, your view of me does seem colored by extreme emotion.

If I were indeed the type you describe, how could I possibly sustain myself writing criticism? Surely it is self-evident that a man who struggles to make chaos of the language of criticism and who displays that struggle in his own writing would be unable to survive no matter how chaotic his surrounding society might be. I believe there is another reason why I have been allowed to exist as a critic. In fact, as I was thinking about this reason, I even hoped that the arrow of your censure would target it. But you cannot see me for what I really am. Your anger clouds your vision.

. . .

Ever since I wrote the essay "Multiple Designs" in *Kaizō*, I have continued to write criticism on the principle that all theories or methods are but designs worn by critics, and that true criticism begins with what is left to be said after one has cast off each and every design. Even today I have not wavered from that fundamental belief. . . . My criticism has been crowned with an array of adjectives: subjective, dogmatic, psychological, irrational, among others. At the level of surface description, perhaps any and all of these adjectives will do. Yet for me, one fact is certain. I always circle about the same place. No matter what direction I set out toward, I suddenly catch myself circling back to this place. By the same place I mean the space where criticism bears witness to the self, or where not bearing self-witness is also possible. I have been prey to a whole range of doubts and convictions over the years, but have always clung to a belief in the fundamental ordinariness of the critic. Whatever the particular method or theory, all issue from this basic principle. It may happen that some theories, even under these conditions, never flower but die in a barren field. I feel such things are inevitable in criticism.

. . .

We have both been damaged by the disorder of our critical language, which possesses neither the universality of technical expression nor the actuality of a local dialect. Neither of us sought to create such chaos; it was a condition visited upon us. We share this common fate. It is time for us to examine our wounds, the damage done by the peculiar nature of this modern Japanese culture. It is no time for the wounded to battle each other.

"Problems of the Modern Novel"

(May 1936)

Just as in any society there are readers from the upper and the lower classes, so too are there higher and lower forms of writing. I suppose it was inevitable that this obvious condition of any culture's life would have become entangled with a condition peculiar to contemporary Japan; namely, the confrontation between pure literature and writing for the masses. As we can see in the fiction of Maupassant, all first-rate writing possesses a popular nature, if only because this popular nature is crucial to the character of the novel. At present, our writers of pure literature tend to equate "popular" with lower-class, whereas writers of mass literature equate it with entertainment. But as the movement to create a more public and broadly social "pure novel" intensifies, and as our pure novelists of today begin to write serially in the newspapers or to publish their serialized pieces as long novels, then pure literature will surely retrieve for itself a robust storytelling element, indeed a "popular" nature. At present, however, our novelists must be painfully aware how difficult it is to retrieve such qualities. Perhaps such pain and strife will breathe new life into pure literature.

"A Study of Kikuchi Kan"

(January 1937)

Of course the sphere is limited, but among the authors whom I know personally, Shiga Naoya and Kikuchi Kan alone, I believe, possess genius. It may sound odd to classify these writers this way, and some may think that my sense of respect toward each of them has clouded my judgment. However, this is how I honestly feel. I believe it is the acuity of Kikuchi and the acuity of Shiga Naoya that together represent the most distinguished literary accomplishment of our time. It is a truly radical acuity they share, leaving no room for conceptual artifice. Few things are as unreliable as the sharpness of the average writer, since it is an occupational hazard to acquire the habit of writing with simulated feeling about things one has no feeling for and to skillfully camouflage one's dulled nerves. I do not find very credible what people call "artistic agony," or "poetic sensitivity," or "a novelist's way of seeing things." And I would not care to estimate how many writers of fake sharpness have been built from weak hearts and mental machinations.

Kikuchi's acuity can seem at times almost pathological. Once he traveled to Hokkaido to give a public lecture and encountered the spirit of a dead woman at the inn where he was staying. As I listened to him recount this experience, stripped of all extraneous details, in a flat, almost bored monotone, I recognized the unusual character of his sensibility. To the degree that he does not quite believe in the spirit of the dead woman, he does not quite believe in the spirit of art. And he speaks about both simply, without embellishment.

. . .

From the outset Kikuchi wrote neither for himself nor for literature. He did not write for critics or for other writers. He became a writer who just wrote for the average reader. Now where the average reader is concerned, no kind of literary or ideological design exists. Still less is any distinction drawn between pure literature and the popular. Such a reader just plunges straight into the work, unarmed, drawn to what is there of human interest.

"The Issue of 'Things Japanese'"

(April 1937)

I must regard this issue of "things Japanese" as but one aspect of the problem of modern anxiety. The pure novel, activism, humanism—one after another such *bundan*-generated problems fade away. Yet the strain and anxiety to establish some new literature runs through them all and has not disappeared. If we focus only on our literary struggles and debates, we see dizzying change. But in actual stories and novels this kind of dizzying change never emerges. At the surface level of critical description, there seems to be constant progress and development. Still, true progress is profoundly slow to arrive. Critics are always waging battles on an immaterial ground. The battle over "things Japanese" is no different.

. . .

Writers are powerless so long as they rely on slogans like "Japanism" or "patriotism." There is not a single example in our literary history of a great work whose greatness was owing to "nationalism." The literary idea of "things Japanese" can be meaningful only if it enables writers to grasp a personal, individual image of something Japanese. To that extent, "things Japanese" is not so much a reactionary idea, as it is an idea fraught with paradox.

"Modern Writers and Style"

(July 1937)

The loss of style is the most striking characteristic of modern literature. The very word "style" has been replaced by the word "observation." Rather than try to write skillfully, everyone tries to see correctly. In short, by replacing a distinctive style with a correct observation, writers have made language a mere mediator between the observer and the observed. Any writer, maturing toward a sense of himself as a writer, will necessarily acquire a distinctive style, but today very little conscious effort is being expended to write distinctively. Thus a strange spectacle presents itself, whereby the difficulties in becoming a real writer remain unchanged, yet almost nothing stands in the way of someone who just wants to declare himself a writer.

. . .

Because the object to be represented—the real world of our times—has no solidity, a hard-edged realism has disappeared from the literary scene. Yet what has not at all disappeared is a deceptive way of thinking about realism carried over from the unreflecting attitudes held by realists all along. Far from not disappearing, the issue of "what we must write" seems to rule the brains of contemporary writers, and so by degrees the deception spreads and magnifies. True enough, today we no longer speak of reading a work of hard-edged realism; instead we claim to be reading *reportage*.

"The Direction of Literary Criticism"

(August 1937)

"Critics are like flies on a horse; the horse should use its tail every so often," Chekhov was once heard to say. It is a simple anec-
dote, about a horse superior to critics who are flies. In our own literary world, many writers are upset with their critics. Sadly, the
reasons for this turmoil remain unclear. No questions are raised
about the deeply disturbing, irrepressibly human disposition to
hallucinate, on the order of a fly who fancies itself a rider, or a pig
who vainly imagines itself a horse. The turmoil between writers
and critics, which repeats itself everyday, has yet to provoke a legit-
imate protest by writers against the misunderstanding of critics.
But there may be something even more troubling at work here. It is
hard to name this "something," although we sense it to be a rotten
something having to do with the ambiguous and deeply festering
relations between writers and critics raised in a literary world that
has been expanding at a furious rate ever since the Taishō period.

To be sure, what we call the modern novel has a shallow tradition in our country, but when we turn to our "tradition" of modern
literary criticism, its shallowness and inconsistencies are of an order that defies contemplation. Perhaps even this generation has yet
to arrive at the point where a thoroughly satisfying criticism can be
written. In the end we may just be providing ballast for future critics to build upon.

Today, people vaguely suppose that the follies of impressionistic criticism have been exposed quite clearly. This is akin to people vaguely supposing that the follies of the I-novel have also been quite clearly revealed. In fact, nothing at all is clear. Just as our so-called *watakushi shōsetsu* is not being discussed in the context of the Western novel of individualism, our impressionistic criticism too is made out to possess an exceedingly impenetrable national character.

. . .

French impressionistic criticism is really sensible criticism. Its origins lay in the *moraliste* tradition traceable to the writings of Montaigne. Regrettably, impressionistic criticism in our country does not possess such an indomitable modern character. And so we face the spectacle of an impoverished criticism, wherein the Naturalist tendencies of [Kosugi] Tengai and [Shimamura] Hōgetsu simply fell in line with a scientific method that was imported along with Marxism.

. . .

With the Taishō period, every manner of opposition to Naturalist writing emerged. Yet criticism, whose style reflected the tastes of Naturalist apologists who would not countenance personal criticism, lost even the seriousness that had marked critical writing heretofore. Writers were preoccupied with certain abstractions—spiritualism, idealism—that represented opposition to Naturalism and with translating these concepts into new fictional techniques. But literary criticism hid itself behind the stylish design called "impressionistic criticism" and made no effort to postulate theories or to reconstruct ideologies. Such work was taken up by philosophers, who were also importing German Idealism at the same time. Yet all these tendencies merely produced an academic clique, isolated from society and cut off from any literary reality. Substantive criticism of literature fell off, even as the literary world itself prospered. This was a phenomenon that might be likened to a wildly popular *go* parlor where each and every bystander offers an amateur's opinion of the game. It is not a particularly amusing analogy, but under such conditions, writers became more loquacious critics than the critics themselves and certainly spoke more cleverly. And the implicit master-servant relationship between writers and critics, maintained within such an environment, has not disappeared even today, when criticism seems to have made such remarkable progress.

Writers who came to maturity in the Taishō period clung to a lingering notion that the critic is really a failed writer. Moreover, this prejudice festered like a congenital illness inside the ordinary, general reader. And so even today, when pure literature is widely spoken of as being on the decline, we see no decrease in the number of aspiring novelists. And even though the significance of criticism is becoming increasingly clear, it remains unthinkable that the number of aspiring critics would increase. The age is over for distinguished fiction, certainly for fiction written intentionally to become "literature." Unfortunately, we witness no fewer literary aspirants, on fire with the conviction that if only they practice writing what seems like fiction, they are bound to produce a real novel. Whenever I meet such aspiring literati, I brace to hear them tell me of their longings to write novels. And I make it a point to first suggest that they study to become critics. So long as there are no true ideals for the young generation to grasp, anyone might aspire to a career in literature, but it will be like placing a bet at the racetrack. . . . Still, all of our writers, both the literary hopefuls and those of proven talent, perpetuate a modern tradition of artless realism, and are marked by its overpowering blood-smell. They try to reach the symbolic from the vantage of the real, without relying on any idealistic, imaginative power, but solely on their "temperament." Marxist literature momentarily provoked shock and uneasiness over the introduction of ideas and concepts to literature, but it did nothing to wash away this smell. Of late our writers find it difficult to produce anything that depends on secondhand ideologies, and so, turning inward toward themselves, they try to reconstruct from there an objective reality. But what rises instead is the stench of a turbid, Japanese-style realism. . . .

Marxist literary criticism was the first to expose our literary world to the fundamental elements of modern criticism, itself an unexpected and unforeseen event. Today we are in a position to recognize and reflect on just what this unforeseen event meant for criticism; namely, the appearance of a method whereby the limits of literature would be determined by social context. Yet this thing called "social context," visited on our *bundan* by an unforeseen and imported, Marxist critical method, was hard for us to envision, caught as we were in the tumult and confusions of the time. In other words, we could not fully account for "modernity," even though it represented our real history. And a history not accounted for will exact its revenge.

. . .

Around the time I left college I began to serialize my first literary review column in *Bungei shunjū*. Having had a smattering of French literature, I was a youth afflicted with the disease of self-confession. For such a youth, the literary review should have been the least accessible of all models of literary expression. Nevertheless, I wrote literary reviews, imagining I could put issues of the self aside and simply converse with others. And I could do this because I had no sense of an audience with whom I might deeply explore the concept of individualism; I was blind also to the reality of the social dimensions of criticism. It is all very well for us to step forward now and admit that indeed, criticism was once practiced in this way. But future historians, examining in detail the actual reviews of the period, won't be able to make sense of them and will abandon all judgment, except perhaps to conjecture that although critical writing proliferated in Japan at this time, the essential character of criticism was lost.

Marxist literary criticism clarified certain social value relations in literary works. It proved variously helpful to writers, although it offered no profound theory of literary aesthetics, being caught up instead in a frenzied politicization of criticism in the name of scientific method. But it was of no benefit to literary critics. The politicization of criticism did bring about a reversal of roles between writers and critics. But there is no reason to think that critics achieved self-conscious independence from writers, just because they claimed to have exchanged a whole range of casual critical methods for one of "guiding principles." After all, there is scant difference between mere enslavement, and falling into the depth of some guiding principle.

. . .

Literature does not abide the kind of deception that is unavoidable in politics. No matter how literary ideas try to accommodate political ideas in a variety of contexts, at a basic level they are irreconcilable. Even a masterpiece cannot kill a fly or satisfy the hunger of a single person. In that sense, the value of literary ideas is not a tangible value, but a symbolic one. It is impossible to think of the activity we call literature apart from a longing for the eternal beyond the actual. The true difficulty of literary criticism lies in this recognition.

. . .

No matter how much common sense is brought to bear on the subject, the world recognizes the artwork and scientific research as different things. Putting aside what the artist and the scientist think about the matter, looking instead at how they go about their labors, we would find each one at work protecting his own special area. But no area is as nebulous as that of the critic who exists between them. The mediating character of literary criticism, its resemblance to both literature and science, might be seen by the outsider as mere ambiguity. Again, the ambiguous nature of certain critical works may provoke feelings of generalized contempt for critics, regardless of their academic or artistic disposition. But ambiguity should not be interpreted so negatively, so long as it is an irrepressible characteristic of the criticism. Essentially, critical consciousness is a spirit torn between scientific analysis and creative desire. It is nothing other than a consciousness in crisis. We might say that it draws inspiration for its work from a sense of equanimity at being in such a dangerous place. Thibaudet once said that "critics who do not criticize critics or the spirit of criticism are but lukewarm critics." It may prove hard to reach this point, but the critic who is not moved always by an arrogant wish to lay hold of a clear image of himself, existing at a point of crisis, will be unable to write truly creative criticism.

"On War"

(November 1937)

I was asked by a certain magazine to discuss my preparation for war in my capacity as a writer. But there can be no special preparation for war that is peculiar to writers. Should the time come to take up arms, I would happily do so and perhaps even die for my country. I can neither conceive of any other preparation for war nor feel there is any need to do so. It is totally meaningless to claim that one would take up arms as a writer. In battle, only soldiers fight.

Literature exists for peace, not for war. In peace a writer can entertain any amount of complexity, but in the vortex of war he can take but one stance. The battle must be won. And, at the moment he realizes that this belief will not be found in any literary theory, a writer should immediately drop literature.

A Life of Dostoevsky

(January 1935–May 1939)

Historians are fond of the expression "History repeats itself."
But we know in our hearts that what happened once will not come
our way again. For that very reason we value the past. History represents on a grand scale the bitterness and regret of humanity. If it
were the case that a given event could be repeated exactly as it occurred, then we would have discovered nothing so profoundly res-
onant as the word *remembrance*. We must understand how deeply
our uncertain lives are bound to specific events, of either our past
or our future, that are unique and unrepeatable. Whether it be our
love, our hate, or our reverence, our feelings are always bound to an
irreplaceable other. Moreover, our desire for such a bond is quite
different from any urge to stereotype humanity, itself a symptom of
our loss of interest in distinct human beings.

No matter how much good fortune we experience on a given day,
we could not bear to live that same day again. Poe's "William Wilson" is not just a tale of the macabre. The author's terror exists
within us all. Just so is it futile to tell the mother who has lost a
child that there are countless mothers like her throughout the
world. The enumeration of comparable losses does nothing but
confirm the incomparable, unique nature of her own loss. The
sense of irreplaceability surrounding this event is commensurate
only with the irreplaceable anguish of the mother. Will we claim

that her tear-filled eyes cloud her judgment? If so, then what do those of us, clear of eye, really see?

What confirms for the mother that the death of her child is a singular, irreplaceable event in history is her very sorrow. This is because in any context, knowledge alone cannot account for what is irreplaceable. The deeper the mother's sorrow, the clearer will her child's face appear before her, perhaps clearer than it ever was in life. And perhaps it is around the mother's heart, framed by the small articles left behind by her beloved child, that we will find the wellspring of whatever wisdom we have about history, whatever will allow us to attend closely to what happened at one time, amid the everyday contingencies of life. Rather than saying this constitutes our basic understanding of historical events, we should say that it represents our basic technique to reach any such understanding. This is because we do not so much see historical facts as they are revealed to us, as we create historical facts out of particular historical materials. In the light of such wisdom, historical facts appear to be neither objective nor subjective. Epistemologically, such wisdom may seem vague or unreliable. But looked upon as an action, it is as certain as our very lives.

. . .

I harbor no ambition to bring the historical person Dostoevsky back to life. Neither do I intend, by means of this subject, to hold forth about myself. Indeed, to indulge oneself in this way, on the premise that one cannot distance oneself from a so-called self, does not represent an excess so much as it does a harmful delusion. Of course neither do I intend to portray Dostoevsky's shape exactly as it was in life. Only a fool would harbor such a desire.

Again, I have no intention to write history by adhering to a fixed method. This is because our everyday experience teaches us that whenever the past quickens toward life, people are actively using their ability to see difference, paradox, and contradiction. All historical materials are but empty husks left behind by those who were once alive. I neither believe in the husks themselves, nor do I indulge a facile belief whereby human character is thought to emerge from a mere gathering of them. The regeneration of human character requires no more nor no less artistry and craft than that of a mother who does not know how to portray the face of her dead child, except through the small articles he left behind or through her deep sorrow. The mother's artistry is minimal, yet it is necessary and basic to the task of any biographer. The real difficulty about treating a complex historical subject is never to forget but to preserve the irreducible simplicity of a mother's artistry.

. . .

Among the bitter potions Dostoevsky drank in his youth was one that made him hypersensitive to the psychology of revolution. Thus, outward appearances notwithstanding, he could grasp the Narodnik revolution of the 1860's for what it was: a mere extension of the radical idealism he had known in the 1840's. He was the first to discern both the sentimentality and the contradictions that generated this revolution. *The Devils*, for example, which has often been labeled a reactionary work, enacts a dissection of revolutionary psychology, indeed a dissection so savage as to be explicable only in terms of the author's vindictiveness. Of course we know that over the years Russian voices have been heard, denouncing Dostoevsky as a reactionary or cursing him as a know-nothing. In our country as well, the champions of the proletarian movement have looked on him with contempt. It would seem that even now the bias against him has not abated in the least. No doubt this bias has been stimulated by a simplistic overestimation of the political significance of his work. Clearly, he opposed the revolutionary Russia of his time. But he did so because his understanding of the Russia of his time far surpassed any nihilist's understanding. Indeed, the shape of the underground movement sketched out in *The Devils* relies to a considerable degree on the author's willingness to caricature himself. Who is there to say that such caricature is not the most effective method to excavate the subconscious deceptions practiced by the nihilists themselves? And, despite the caricature, it is clear that Dostoevsky never took the nihilist position lightly.

. . .

The word *narod* is a very old one in Russian, corresponding to the word "people" in English. It connotes rather vaguely the public or the masses. Only later was the foreign term *natsia* brought into the language, bearing the meaning of "nation." And so the Narodnik movement was not a nationalist movement, strictly speaking, but a populist one. In the intellectual climate of the 1840's, when the intelligentsia began its ideological battles, it split into a patriotic camp and a progressive camp, although both equally referred to Western models to justify their actions. Again, both camps were afflicted by the vagueness of the word *narod*. And so alongside their concepts of a modern nation or a modern people, appeared a vision common to them both, of unenlightened peasants spreading across the plains without end. While the progressives and the xenophobes were thus waging their fierce debates, they remained mutually ignorant of what provoked their battle in the first place; namely, the proper dimensions of this *narod*-like creature, which as a vague abstraction could be neither friend nor foe, nor responsive to any movement. From that period forward, the Russian intelligentsia has been shadowed by this phantom *narod*.

· · ·

Before Dostoevsky's eyes, always, were the people. But did the people actually exist? The Russian people whom he addressed with such power were of course Russian peasants. But did any peasants appear clearly before his eyes? As we know, ordinary peasants do not figure in his work. What surer proof exists that Dostoevsky had no real knowledge of peasant life? As an artist, he unflinchingly confessed that the peasants were, in the end, unknown and a puzzle to him. What then was alive in his work? A word; the word *narod*. And this word seemed as vital as any person he could see or touch.

REFERENCE MATTER

Glossary

Akutagawa Ryūnosuke (1892–1927), short-story writer, essayist, chronicler of the pathological and the perverse.

Barres, Maurice (1862–1923), French novelist and nationalist politician; apologist for the supremacy of the individual.

Bourget, Paul (1852–1935), French novelist; his *Le Disciple* (1889; trans. 1901) details the ruin of a student who applies Naturalistic literary theories to life.

bundan (literary world), conventionally used to describe the small group of writers, critics, and editors whose work and opinions have determined what qualifies as "literature" throughout the modern period.

bungei fukkō (literary revival), describes a movement in the mid-1930's, when progressive or subversive literature was suppressed, and the values of the classics or of "pure Japanese" culture were advanced.

Bungei shunjū (1923–), literary and general-interest magazine of wide circulation, founded by Kikuchi Kan.

chambara, a type of period film featuring sword fighting.

Chesterton, Gilbert Keith (1874–1936), English author; conservative apologist and prolific commentator on economic and literary issues.

Chikamatsu Shūkō (1876–1944), Naturalist writer, known for his confessional tales of betrayal and humiliation.

Chūō kōron (1887–), a leading magazine of cultural and political opinion.

Constant, Benjamin (1767–1830), French-Swiss political writer and novelist; author of the introspective, highly personal novel *Adolphe* (1816).

Dostoevsky, Feodor Mikhailovich (1821–81), Russian novelist; subject of Kobayashi's longest prewar study, *A Life of Dostoevsky.*

Edokko (child of Edo), connoting both one's birth and upbringing in the capital city, and nostalgia for the urban chic of Edo, as Tokyo was once called.

Etō Jun (1933–), literary scholar and critic, famous for his studies of Sōseki and Kobayashi.

France, Anatole (1844–1924), French writer; allegorist and, beginning with *Le livre de mon ami* (1913), author of several autobiographical novels.

Friche, Vladimir Maksimovich (1870–1929), art and literary historian; an early practitioner of the theory of dialectical materialism and supporter of the Bolshevik revolution.

furoshiki, a piece of cloth used to bundle and carry small items.

Futabatei Shimei (1864–1909), novelist, Russian translator; famous for his pioneering translations of Turgenev, and for writing the "first" modern novel, *Ukigumo* (1887–89).

gendaimono (modern piece), films or plays about contemporary life; to be distinguished from work set in the past, on historical subjects or themes (*jidaimono*).

Gide, André (1869–1951), French writer; valued in Japan especially for his autobiographical works.

giri-ninjō (duty vs. desire), particularly descriptive of dramatic tension in the kabuki and puppet theater since the seventeenth century.

Goethe, Johann Wolfgang von (1749–1832), German writer and scientist; his *Sorrows of Young Werther* was especially influential in Japan near the turn of the twentieth century.

Gourmont, Remy de (1858–1915), French critic and novelist; advocate of Symbolism and other modern literary forms.

Gundolf, Friedrich (1880–1931), German literary scholar, known especially for his philosophical studies of Shakespeare and the German spirit, and of Goethe.

Hayashi Fusao (1903–75), novelist and essayist; among the more famous of 1930's "ideological converts," turning from leftist to rightist themes.

Hiratsuka Raichō (1886–1971), feminist author and founder of the journal *Seitō.*

Hirotsu Kazuo (1891–1968), novelist and critic; known for his defense of prose realism and his studies of Tolstoy and Shiga.

Ibuse Masuji (1898–1993), novelist, best known for *Black Rain,* an account of suffering and survival after the bombing of Hiroshima.

Ihara Saikaku (1642–1693), early Edo writer of *haikai* verse and comic tales on the theme of money and sex; parodist of traditional conventions and observer of merchant life.

Ikuta Chōkō (1882–1936), critic of eclectic tastes and allegiance; resisted Naturalism and proletarian writing; translator of Nietzsche.

Ishibashi Ningetsu (1865–1926), German scholar and one of the first Meiji literary critics.

Ishikawa Takuboku (1886–1912), poet and essayist; brilliant innovator of modern *tanka*.

Iwanami Bunko, refers to Iwanami's "library" of inexpensive editions devoted to modern authors, begun in 1927; one popular line presented translations of foreign writing.

Janet, Pierre (1859–1947), French physician and psychologist; known for his early studies of hysteria and hypnosis.

jidaimono (period piece), films or plays with a historical subject or setting; to be distinguished in the twentieth century from work with a modern setting (*gendaimono*).

junbungaku (pure literature), especially since the 1920's, a type of personal or confessional prose, as opposed to popular or proletarian writing.

Kaizō (Reconstruction), a monthly general interest magazine (April 1919–February 1955), originally committed to an agenda of social reform; published a broad range of critical controversy and fiction.

Kamo no Chōmei (1155–1216), poet and essayist; author of the famous meditation on suffering and reclusion from the world, *Hōjōki* (An account of my hut).

Kamura Isota (1897–1933), short-story writer; known for his confessional portraits of betrayal and misery, as drawn from his own or other writers' lives.

Kawabata Yasunari (1899–1972), novelist; known for his early experimental fiction and for his later, lyrical prose; first Japanese winner of the Nobel Prize for Literature (1968).

Kawakami Tetsutarō (1902–70), wide-ranging critic of music and poetry; scholar of Dostoevsky and Lev Shestov; portraitist of such modern iconoclasts as Nakahara Chūya, Ōsugi Sakae, Okakura Tenshin, and Yoshida Shōin.

Kikuchi Kan (1888–1948), novelist, playwright, editor; advocate both of popular fiction and of better compensation for professional writers; ardent nationalist.

Kitamura Tōkoku (1868–94), poet and critic; known as leader of the Romantics associated with the magazine *Bungakkai*.

Kōda Rohan (1867–1947), novelist, playwright, essayist; one of the great Meiji literary reformers, noted for his defense of Saikaku and other, spiritual elements of the Japanese past.

kokyō, the place of one's birth; ancestral home.

Kosugi Tengai (1865–1952), novelist; regarded as a precursor of the Naturalists in his treatment of common life and social themes.

Kume Masao (1891–1952), author of both pure and popular fiction; widely known for his defense of Japanese personal fiction, against the expansive style of a Dostoevsky or Balzac.

Kunikida Doppo (1871–1908), poet and short-story writer; heralded as a precursor of the Naturalists.

Lemaitre, Jules (1853–1914), French critic, known for his impressionistic style.

magemono (lit., top-knot piece), stories or plays about samurai or *rōnin*; more broadly, twentieth-century vehicles to convey the manners and mores of premodern Japan.

Mallarmé, Stephane (1842–98), French poet and leader of the Symbolists; profoundly influential in the development of modern Japanese poetry and poetics.

Man'yōshū (Collection of ten thousand leaves), first great collection of Japanese verse (ca. 759), containing the earliest poems in the language; frequently cited by writers looking for the "original" voice of Japanese poetry.

Marx, Karl (1818–93), German social philosopher, whose books and ideas were translated and dominated intellectual discussion in Japan during the 1920's and early 1930's.

Masamune Hakuchō (1879–1962), Naturalist short-story writer, playwright, critic; acerbic reviewer of contemporary Japanese writing, stressing serious over light fiction.

Matsuo Bashō (1644–1694), legendary or famous poet and prose writer, notably of haiku and travel diaries.

Maupassant, Guy de (1850–93), French novelist and short-story writer; especially influential on the Japanese Naturalists.

Mérimée, Prosper (1803–70), French author of plays, ballads, novellas, and historical studies; noted for the concision and understatement of his prose.

Miki Kiyoshi (1897–1945), philosopher, cultural critic; trained in both Heidegarrian and Marxist thought; associated with Nishida Kitarō and the Kyoto School.

Mita-ha, refers to the group of writers, including Ōgai and Kafū, associated with the magazine *Mita bungaku* (1910–25), known for their early resistance to Naturalist fiction.

Miyamoto Kenji (1908–?), prominent Marxist critic and politician; author of "Literature of Defeat," a study of Akutagawa.

Mori Ōgai (1862–1922), an army doctor and one of the most influential of modern writers; German scholar, translator, editor, author of lyrical romances, historical fiction, and family chronicles; as a critic, stressed the difference between art and life.

Morocco (1930), a Josef von Sternberg Hollywood talkie, starring Marlene Dietrich; one of the first foreign films to be screened in Japan using subtitles and not live narration.

Motoori Norinaga (1730–1801), poet and scholar of "national learning"; greatest premodern critic, whose studies range from *The Tale of Genji* to the *Man'yōshū*.

Nagai Kafū (1879–1959), novelist, essayist; known for his lyrical evocations of a vanishing Tokyo and for portrayals of its demimonde.

Nakahara Chūya (1907–37), poet; strongly influenced, in his life and art, by Rimbaud and the Dadaists.

Nakamura Mitsuo (1911–?), critic; known for his fiction studies of Maupassant, Flaubert, and Futabatei, and for his critique of Naturalism and the I-novel.

Nakano Shigeharu (1902–79), prominent Marxist novelist, poet, and critic.

Natsume Sōseki (1867–1916), Chinese and English scholar, novelist and critic, regarded by many as the greatest writer of modern Japan; his late novels especially reveal the pressures and tragedies of modern life.

Naturalism, refers to the influential literary movement, often dated from Tayama Katai's *Futon* (The quilt; 1907), that featured confessional realism on such themes as betrayal and displacement; notable Naturalists include Katai, Shimazaki Tōson, Tokuda Shūsei, and Chikamatsu Shūkō.

Nerval, Gérard de (1808–55), French poet and fantasy writer, regarded as a precursor of the modern surrealists.

Nietzsche, Friedrich Wilhelm (1844–1900), German philosopher; introduced in Japan near the turn of the century and heralded for his ideas on beauty and aesthetics.

Nogi Marusuke (1849–1912), army general; committed suicide following the death of the Meiji emperor.

Ōsugi Sakae (1885–1923), anarchist critic, founder of the journal *Kindai shisō* (Modern thought); murdered in police custody following the earthquake of 1923.

Ozaki Kōyō (1867–1903), novelist; urbane stylist in the tradition of Saikaku, and highly influential literary patron of Izumi Kyōka, Higuchi Ichiyō, and other Meiji authors.

Pater, Walter Horatio (1839–94), English essayist and critic; apologist for an aestheticization of life.

Plekhanov, Georgij Valentinovich (1856–1918), Russian revolutionary and social philosopher who helped introduce Marxism to Russia.

Poe, Edgar Allan (1809–49), American poet, short-story writer, and critic; noted for his artistic daring and desperate life, and in Japan, for being admired by the French, especially Baudelaire.

Proust, Marcel (1871–1922), French novelist; by the early 1930's, he and James Joyce were regarded as the leading modernists.

Ribot, Théodule (1839–1916), French psychologist; wrote on the effects of heredity and personality disorders.

Rimbaud, Arthur (1854–91), French poet, heralded as one of the first great Symbolists; widely translated and discussed in Japan from the 1920's.

Romanticism, in Japan, first associated with the poet Kitamura Tō-koku and the magazine *Bungakkai* in the 1890's, where such foreign Romantics as Rousseau, Byron, Wordsworth, along with proponents of German Idealism, were translated and widely discussed.

Rousseau, Jean-Jacques (1712–78), Swiss-French author and composer; theorist of a "good" human nature corrupted by civilization; noted in Japan especially for the autobiographical *Confessions*.

Rugé, Arnold (1803–80), German philosopher; Hegelian aesthetician; social activist and early proponent of Marxist thought.

Ruttman, Walter (1887–1941), German director, known especially for his documentaries of Berlin and his *World Melody* (1929); later an adviser to Leni Riefenstahl in the editing of her *Olympia* (1938).

Sainte-Beuve, Charles Augustin (1804–69), French literary historian and critic.

Sanetomo (Minamoto Sanetomo; 1192–1219), the third Kamakura shogun and an admired poet.

Satō Haruo (1892–1964), poet, novelist, critic; known especially as a Taishō period decadent, whose later writings reflect a more traditionalist, nativist "return."

Sénancour, Etienne Pivert de (1770–1846), French writer, especially identified with his autobiographical novel, *Obermann* (1804), said to reflect the influence of Rousseau.

Shiga Naoya (1883–1971), novelist, member of the Shirakaba school; author of the most famous of all Japanese I-novels, *Anya kōro* (A dark night's passing), written between 1921 and 1937.

Shigarami zōshi, influential Meiji period literary magazine (March 1889–August 1894); notable both for the editorial leadership of Mori Ōgai, and for encouraging literary criticism and theory.

Shimamura Hōgetsu (1871–1918), critic, dramatist, English scholar, translator; known especially as an early champion of Naturalism.

Shimazaki Tōson (1872–1943), poet, Naturalist writer; known for his modern, Romantic verse and for his confessional novels, especially the early *Hakai* (Broken commandment; 1906).

Shinkankaku-ha (Neo-Perceptionist school), modernist literary group, active in the 1920's, led by Yokomitsu Riichi and Kawabata Yasunari; concerned with the sensations generated by urban living, prior to any moral or political analysis.

shinkyō shōsetsu ("environment of feeling" fiction), a lyrical, quietistic form of I-novel that was especially popular in the 1920's.

Shinshichō (Tide of new thought), literary magazine, founded in 1907; propagated decadent writing as an antidote to Naturalism.

Shirakaba-ha (White Birch Society), the group and its magazine were at the center of Taishō period culture; advocated a cosmopolitan individualism, and fiction "true" to the writer's life; notable members include Mushanokōji Saneatsu, Shiga Naoya, and Arishima Takeo.

Symons, Arthur (1865–1945), English poet, translator, and critic; leading figure of the Symbolists in England, chiefly known for *The Symbolist Movement in Literature* (1899).

Taine, Hippolyte-Adolphe (1828–93), French critic and historian; analyzed the effects of heredity and environment on culture; associated with the Naturalists.

Takayama Chogyū (1871–1902), Romantic critic; echoed both Norinaga and Nietzsche in valuing aesthetics over morals in literature.

Takeda Rintarō (1904–46), novelist, born in Osaka; known for his portraits of city life and the lower classes.

Takii Kōsaku (1894–?), novelist and poet; disciple of Shiga Naoya, noted for his late pastoral fiction.

Tanizaki Jun'ichirō (1886–1965), Tokyo-born novelist, famous for his stylistic virtuosity and tales of decadent desire.

Tayama Katai (1871–1930), Naturalist writer, noted for his early novel *Futon* (The quilt; 1907), about a writer's scandalous love; advocate of gritty prose.

Tempyō age, strictly, the era 729–49; more generally, refers to the art and culture of the latter half of the Nara period (710–93).

tenkō (conversion), specifically the "ideological conversion" of Marxist or progressive writers, under government pressure in the 1930's.

Thibaudet, Albert (1874–1936), French literary critic; student of Bergson and early supporter of the Symbolists.

Tokuda Shūsei (1871–1943), Naturalist writer, born in Kanazawa; his novels depict the lives of common people adrift in urban life; known especially for his portrayals of women.

Tosaka Jun (1900–1945), philosopher, critic; foremost theoretician of dialectical materialism before and during the war years.

Tsubouchi Shōyō (1859–1935), Meiji novelist, English scholar, translator, and critic; argued for a new, more realistic type of novel.

Uchida Roan (1868–1929), critic, novelist, and translator; advocate of social and political novels, and the realism of such Western writers as Dostoevsky, Tolstoy, Zola, and Dickens.

Ueda Bin (1874–1916), poet, critic, translator, notably of French Symbolism.

Uno Kōji (1891–1961), novelist, especially of eccentric, experimental I-novels.

Valéry, Paul (1871–1945), French poet and critic; a follower of the Symbolists; influential in Japan from the 1920's.

Verlaine, Paul (1844–1896), French poet; an early Symbolist; known in Japan for his bohemian, decadent artist's life.

Waseda bungaku, literary magazine, begun in 1891 under the direction of Tsubouchi Shōyō and, later, Shimamura Hōgetsu; mainstay of the Naturalist movement.

Waseda-ha, the group of writers, including Shōyō and Hōgetsu, associated with the literary magazine *Waseda bungaku*; known for their early support of Naturalist writing.

watakushi shōsetsu, the Japanese "I-novel"; dominant form of modern fiction since the Taishō period.

Wordsworth, William (1770–1850), English poet; first-generation Romantic, widely translated in Japan by the turn of the twentieth century.

Yamaji Aizan (1864–1917), journalist, critic; apologist for utilitarian forms of writing.

Yasuda Yojūrō (1910–81), leading Romantic critic during the 1930's; known for his studies of German aesthetics and traditional Japanese culture.

Yazaki Dan (1906–46), critic; associated with the "literary revival" of the mid-1930's; probed issues of modernity, the self, and Japanese tradition.

Yokomitsu Riichi (1898–1947), novelist; founder of the Neo-Perceptionist movement in the 1920's; early, experimental fiction; by the late 1930's, turned to more traditional styles and themes; as a critic, advocated literature that combined the pure and popular.

zadankai, the published transcription of a roundtable discussion held among leading writers or critics, popular throughout the twentieth century.

Zeami (Kanze Motokiyo; 1364–1443), actor, playwright, and critic; with his father, Kan'ami, founded the Nō theater.

Chronology

1902   born April 11 in the Kanda district of Tokyo

1921   father dies in March; Kobayashi matriculates to the First Normal School (Ikkō) in April

1925   enters the French literature department of Tokyo Imperial University; meets the poet Nakahara Chūya

1926   earliest criticism, "Rimbaud I," appears in the French department's literary magazine

1928   graduates from the university with a thesis on Rimbaud. Lives for a time in Nara

1929   returns to Tokyo in the Spring; publishes "Multiple Designs" in September; first study of Shiga

1930   active as literary reviewer for *Bungei shunjū*; publishes translation of Rimbaud's *Une Saison en enfer*; study of Yokomitsu

1931   first book of critical writings published under the title *Bungei hyōron*; moves to Kamakura

1932   appointed part-time instructor of literature at Meiji University; study of Valéry; "Anxiety and Modern Literature"

1933   May, "Literature of the Lost Home"; with Hayashi Fusao, Takeda Rintarō, and Kawabata, founds literary magazine *Bungakkai* (Oct.)

1934   January, "Chaos in the Literary World"; marries in May; first study of Dostoevsky appears

1935   January, becomes editor of *Bungakkai*; begins serial publication of "Discourse on Fiction of the Self" and *A Life of Dostoevsky*

1936	carries on debates in print with Masamune Hakuchō, Nakano Shigeharu, and Tosaka Jun, on issues of art and life, tradition and modernity
1937	"A Study of Kikuchi Kan"; "The Direction of Literary Criticism"; "On War"; daughter born in March
1938	February, "A Study of Shiga Naoya"; travels to China as a correspondent for *Bungei shunjū*
1939	*A Life of Dostoevsky* published by Sōgensha in May
1940	Lectures in Korea and Manchuria
1941	serial essays on "History and Literature," Pascal's *Pensées*, and *The Brothers Karamazov*
1942	begins essays on medieval literature: "On Evanescence," "*The Tale of the Heike*," "Sanetomo," "Saigyō," "*Essays in Idleness*"
1943	leaves for China in December as part of the Greater East Asian Writers Assembly; begins his writings on Mozart
1946	February, Sōgensha publishes the collection, *On Evanescence*; mother dies in May; *Kindai bungaku* roundtable on Kobayashi; resigns from Meiji University
1948	book publication of *On "Crime and Punishment"*; first study of van Gogh appears
1953	*The Letters of van Gogh* awarded Yomiuri Prize; travels through Europe
1954	March, begins serialization of *Modern Painters*
1958	April, publication of *Modern Painters*; series of essays on Bergson begins in May
1959	named member of the Arts Academy; occasional essays titled "Hints for Thinking," "Common Sense" appear
1963	invited to the Soviet Union; travels through Europe
1965	begins serialization of *Motoori Norinaga* in June (*Shinchō*); grandchild born
1967	awarded the Medal of Culture
1977	*Motoori Norinaga* published by Shinchōsha in the fall
1978	newly revised *Kobayashi Hideo zenshū*, edited by Ōoka Shōhei, Nakamura Mitsuo, and Etō Jun, published by Shinchōsha
1983	dies on March 1

Bibliography

Works by Kobayashi Hideo
(listed in order of appearance)

PART I: COMPLETE WORKS

The translations in this section are complete and unabridged renderings of texts found in the standard edition of Kobayashi's collected works, *Kobayashi Hideo zenshū* (15 vols., Shinchōsha, 1979). Besides English and Japanese titles, and identification of the relevant *KHZ* text, the original date and place of publication is given in brackets. Kobayashi often revised his work prior to its *zenshū* publication. In most cases the changes are of minor, chiefly stylistic consequence. In a few places following the translations, I have noted where a more significant change has been made.

"Multiple Designs" ("Samazama naru ishō"). *KHZ* 1: 11–27 [*Kaizō*, Sept. 1929].
"The Anxiety of Modern Literature" ("Gendai bungaku no fuan"). *KHZ* 1: 145–54 [*Kaizō*, June 1932].
"Literature of the Lost Home" ("Kokyō o ushinatta bungaku"). *KHZ* 3: 29–37 [*Bungei shunjū*, May 1933].
"Chaos in the Literary World" ("Bungakkai no konran"). *KHZ* 3: 50–61 [*Bungei shunjū*, Jan. 1934].
"Discourse on Fiction of the Self" ("Watakushi shōsetsu ron"). *KHZ* 3: 119–45 [*Keizai ōrai*, May–Aug. 1935].

PART II: MISCELLANEOUS WRITINGS

This section contains partial translations of early essays, reviews, and one work of fiction, spanning the period 1924–39, with two exceptions: "Recollections of Nakahara Chūya" and "Rimbaud III" are later, retrospective statements on Kobayashi's encounter with these poets in the 1920's.

"One Brain" ("Hitotsu no nōzui"). *KHZ* 2: 16 [*Seidō jidai*, June 1924].

"Recollections of Nakahara Chūya" ("Nakahara Chūya no omoide"). *KHZ* 2: 125–26 [*Bungei*, Aug. 1949].

"Rimbaud I." *KHZ* 2: 138 [*Furansu bungaku kenkyū*, Oct. 1, 1926].

"Rimbaud II." *KHZ* 2: 149 [*Shijin*, Feb. 1930].

"Rimbaud III." *KHZ* 2: 152, 159, 161, 167 [*Tenbō*, Mar. 1947].

"The Muse and the Fate of Akutagawa Ryūnosuke" ("Akutagawa Ryūnosuke no bishin to shukumei"). *KHZ* 2: 39–40 [*Daichōwa*, Oct. 1927].

"An Approach to *Flowers of Evil*" ("*Aku no hana* ichimen"). *KHZ* 2: 49 [*Furansu bungaku kenkyū*, Nov. 1927].

"Shiga Naoya." *KHZ* 4: 21 [*Shisō*, Dec. 1929]; "A Study of Shiga Naoya" ("Shiga Naoya ron"). *KHZ* 4: 104, 107–8, 113, 115, 116, 117 [*Kaizō*, Feb. 1938].

"On Theory and Practice" ("Ashiru to kame no ko"). *KHZ* 1: 28, 35, 38, 42, 47–48, 56, 58 [*Bungei shunjū*, Apr., May, July 1930].

"Is Literature Unreal?" ("Bungaku wa esoragota ka"). *KHZ* 1: 72, 76 [*Bungei shunjū*, Sept. 1930].

"Yokomitsu Riichi." *KHZ* 1: 82, 88 [*Bungei shunjū*, Nov. 1930].

"A Passion for Materiality" ("Busshitsu e no jōnetsu"). *KHZ* 1: 90–91, 95 [*Bungei shunjū*, Dec. 1930].

"Marx's Insight" ("Marukusu no gotatsu"). *KHZ* 1: 106–7 [*Bungei shunjū*, Jan. 1931].

"Disqualified as a Critic" ("Hihyōka shikkaku"). *KHZ* 1: 168, 173 [*Shinchō*, Nov. 1930]. *KHZ* 1: 178 [*Kaizō*, Feb. 1931].

"On the Work of Ibuse Masuji" ("Ibuse Masuji no sakuhin ni tsuite"). *KHZ* 4: 33–34 [original publication unknown; original MS dated Feb. 1931].

"The Psychological Novel" ("Shinri shōsetsu"). *KHZ* 1: 122–23 [*Bungei shunjū*, Mar. 1931].

"The Debate on the Scientific Nature of Literary Criticism" ("Bungei hihyō no kagakusei ni kansuru ronsō"). *KHZ* 1: 127, 130 [*Shinchō*, Apr. 1931].

"Tanizaki Jun'ichirō." *KHZ* 1: 294, 298, 300 [*Chūō kōron*, May 1931].

"French Literature and the New Japanese Literature" ("Furansu bungaku to wagakuni no shinbungaku"). *KHZ* 1: 196–97 [*Shinchō*, July 1931].

"On Pure Fiction" ("Junsui shōsetsu to iu mono ni tsuite"). *KHZ* 1: 200, 201 [*Bungaku*, Dec. 1931].

"On Valéry" ("Vareii no koto"). *KHZ* 2: 304 [original publication unknown; original MS dated May 1932].

"On Paradox" ("Gyakusetsu to iu mono ni tsuite"). *KHZ* 1: 211–12, 213 [*Yomiuri shimbun*, June 8–10, 1932; originally titled "Bungaku zakkan-gyakusetsu to iu mono ni tsuite"].

"Fiction Studies I." *KHZ* 3: 11, 12, 15 [*Shinchō*, June 1932].

"Letter to X" ("X e no tegami"). *KHZ* 2: 85, 91, 92 [*Chūō kōron*, Sept. 1932].

"Notebook II" ("Techō II"). *KHZ* 1: 264 [*Bungei shunjū*, Mar. 1933].

"On Literary Criticism" ("Bungaku hihyō ni tsuite"). *KHZ* 1: 238 [*Bungaku*, Apr. 1933].

"Tanizaki Jun'ichirō's *Primer on Style*" ("Tanizaki Jun'ichirō *Bunshō tokuhon*"). *KHZ* 4: 50–51 [*Bungakkai*, Jan. 1935].

"More Thoughts on the Literary Review" ("Futatabi bungei jihyō ni tsuite"). *KHZ* 3: 118 [*Kaizō*, Mar. 1935].

"Yokomitsu Riichi's *Book of Remembrance*" ("Yokomitsu Riichi *Oboegaki*"). *KHZ* 4: 53 [unpublished, undated MS; likely written near the time of *Oboegaki*'s publication, June 1935].

"Face of the Author" ("Sakka no kao"). *KHZ* 4: 153 [*Yomiuri shimbun*, Jan. 24–25, 1936].

"Ideas and Real Life" ("Shisō to jisseikatsu"). *KHZ* 4: 166–67 [*Bungei shunjū*, Apr. 1936].

"A Response to Nakano Shigeharu" ("Nakahara Shigeharu kun e"). *KHZ* 4: 168, 169–70, 171 [*Tokyo hibi shimbun*, Apr. 2–3, 1936].

"Problems of the Modern Novel" ("Gendai shōsetsu no shomondai"). *KHZ* 3: 162 [*Chūō kōron*, May 1936].

"A Study of Kikuchi Kan" ("Kikuchi Kan ron"). *KHZ* 4: 87, 93 [*Chūō kōron*, Jan. 1937].

"The Issue of 'Things Japanese'" (" 'Nihonteki na mono' no mondai"). *KHZ* 4: 192, 194 [*Tōkyō Asahi shimbun*, Apr. 16–19, 1937].

"Modern Writers and Style" ("Gendai sakka to buntai"). *KHZ* 4: 238–39, 240 [*Tōkyō Asahi shimbun*, July 17–20, 1937].

"The Direction of Literary Criticism" ("Bungei hihyō no yukikata"). *KHZ* 3: 166–67, 168, 169–70, 171, 179, 181 [*Chūō kōron*, Aug. 1937].

"On War" ("Sensō ni tsuite"). *KHZ* 4: 288 [*Kaizō*, Nov. 1937].

A Life of Dostoevsky (*Dostoevsky no seikatsu*). *KHZ* 5: 15–16, 21, 147–48, 163–64, 165–66 [*Bungakkai*, Jan. 1935–Mar. 1937; Preface, Parts I and II in *Bungakkai*, Oct. 1938; Parts III–V in *Bungei*, May 1939].

Secondary Works Consulted

Aeba Takao. *Kobayashi Hideo to sono jidai*. Bungei shunjū, 1986.

Akiyama Susumu. *Tamashii to isho*. Kōdansha, 1985.

Bakhtin, Mikhail. *Problems of Dostoevsky's Poetics*. Ed. and trans. by Caryl Emerson. Minneapolis: University of Minnesota Press, 1984.

Barshay, Andrew E. *State and Intellectual in Imperial Japan*. Berkeley: University of California Press, 1988.

Benjamin, Walter. *Illuminations*. Ed. and with an Introduction by Hannah Arendt. New York: Schocken Books, 1969.

———. *Reflections*. Ed. and with an Introduction by Peter Demetz. New York: Schocken Books, 1986.

Bungakkai. Special issue on the death of Kobayashi Hideo. May 1983.

Bungaku. Special issue on Kobayashi Hideo. Dec. 1987.

Doak, Kevin Michael. *Dreams of Difference: The Japan Romantic School and the Crisis of Modernity*. Berkeley: University of California Press, 1994.

Etō Jun. *Kobayashi Hideo*. Kōdansha, 1961.

Gide, André. *The Counterfeiters*. New York: Modern Library, 1973.

Haruyama Yukio. "Inshō hihyō no ittenkei." *Mita bungaku*, Oct. 1931.

Hashikawa Bunzo. "Shakaika shita watakushi o megutte—puroretariya bungaku no zasetsu to Kobayashi Hideo." *Bungaku*, Oct. 1958.

Hashimoto Minoru. *Kobayashi Hideo hihan*. Tōjusha, 1980.

Hirano Ken. *Bungaku—Shōwa jūnen zengo*. Bungei shunjū, 1972.

Honda Shūgo. "Kobayashi Hideo ron." *Kindai bungaku*, Apr. 1946.

Ishikawa Takuboku. "Jidai heisoku no genjō." In *Kindai bungaku hyōron takei*, vol. 3. Kadokawa shoten, 1971.

Isoda Koichi. *Shōwa sakkaron shūsei*. Shinchōsha, 1985.

Issatsu no koza—Kobayashi Hideo. Nihon no kindai bungaku, 7. Yūseidō, 1984.

Karatani Kōjin and Nakagami Kenji. *Kobayashi Hideo o koete*. Kawade shobō, 1979.

Karatani Kōjin et al. *Kindai Nihon no hihyō*. Fukutake shoten, 1990.

Keene, Donald. "Kobayashi Hideo." In *Dawn to the West* (Japanese Literature of the Modern Era—Poetry, Drama, Criticism). New York: Holt, Rinehart and Winston, 1984.

Kindai bungaku hyōron taikei. 9 vols. Kadokawa shoten, 1971.

Kokubungaku kaishaku to kanshō, vol. 40. "Kobayashi Hideo no michinori." Aug. 1975.

———. Special issue: Kobayashi Hideo no sekai. June 1993.

Miura Masashi. "Kiki to jōshiki" (Kobayashi Hideo to gendai). *Shinchō*, Apr. 1984.

————. "Kobayashi Hideo wa owatta ka." Special issue: Sengō no bungaku ronsō. *Gunzō*, Sept. 1986.

Miyamoto Kenji. "Kobayashi Hideo ron." *Kaizō*, Dec. 1931.

Nakamura Mitsuo. Afterword: "Hito to bungaku." In *Kobayashi Hideo shū*. Gendai bungaku taikei, vol. 42. Chikuma shobō, 1965.

Nakano Shigeharu. "Bungaku ni okeru shinkanryōshugi." *Shinchō*, Mar. 1937.

Nihon bungaku kenkyū shiryō sōsho. *Kobayashi Hideo*. Yūseidō, 1977.

Noguchi Takehiko. *Bunka kigō to shite no buntai*. Perikan sha, 1987.

Rousseau, Jean-Jacques. *The Confessions*. Trans. and with an Introduction by J. M. Cohen. Middlesex, Eng.: Penguin Books, 1954.

Saeki Shoichi. *Jiden no seiki*. Kōdansha, 1985.

Satō Shizuo. "'Kindai no chōkoku' to gendai bungaku." *Zenei*, Mar. 1984.

Seidensticker, Edward G. "Kobayashi Hideo." In Robert Shively, ed., *Tradition and Modernization in Japanese Culture*. Princeton: Princeton University Press, 1971.

Shima Hiroyuki. *"Kanso" to iu janru*. Chikuma shobō, 1989.

Shinchō. Special issue in memory of Kobayashi Hideo. Apr. 1983.

Shinchō Nihon bungaku arubamu, vol. 31. *Kobayashi Hideo*. Shinchōsha, 1980.

Shōwa hihyō taikei, vols. 1 and 2. Banchō shobō, 1968.

Silverberg, Miriam. *Changing Song: The Marxist Manifestos of Nakano Shigeharu*. Princeton: Princeton University Press, 1990.

Sontag, Susan. *A Barthes Reader*. New York: Hill and Wang, 1982.

Takeda Seijun. *Sekai to iu hairi*. Kawade shobō, 1988.

Tosaka Jun. "Bungei hyōronka no ideorogi." *Kaizō*, Aug. 1933.

Valéry, Paul. *Selected Writings*. New York: New Directions, 1964.

Yamamoto Shichihei. *Kobayashi Hideo no ryūgi*. Shinchōsha, 1986.

Yoshida Hiroo. *Rekuwiemu Kobayashi Hideo*. Kōdansha, 1983.

Yoshimoto Takaaki. "Kobayashi Hideo no hōhō." *Kaishaku to kanshō*, Nov. 1961.

Yuriika. Special issue: Kobayashi Hideo: hihyō to wa nani ka. Oct. 1974.

Index of Names

In this index an "f" after a number indicates a separate reference on the next page, and an "ff" indicates separate references on the next two pages. A continuous discussion over two or more pages is indicated by a span of page numbers, e.g., "57–59." *Passim* is used for a cluster of references in close but not consecutive sequence.

Library of Congress Cataloging-in-Publication Data

Kobayashi, Hideo, 1902–83
[Selections. English. 1995]
Literature of the lost home : Kobayashi Hideo—literary criticism,
1924–1939 / edited and translated and with an introduction by
Paul Anderer.
p.   cm.
Translation of selected works from: Kobayashi Hideo zenshū
(15 vols., Shinchōsha, 1979).
Includes bibliographical references.
ISBN 0-8047-2537-3 (cl.) : ISBN 0-8047-4115-8 (pbk.)
1. Kobayashi, Hideo, 1902–   —Translations into English.
2. Japanese literature—History and criticism.   3. Criticism.
I. Anderer, Paul.   II. Title.
PL832.O28A22   1995
809—dc20
94-49638 CIP

⊗ Printed on recycled, acid-free paper.

Original printing 1995
First paperback printing 2000
Last figure below indicates year of this printing:
08   07   06   05   04   03   02   01   00